Milan Jesih:
Selected Poems

Translated from the Slovenian
by Nada Grošelj

T0161827

DALKEY ARCHIVE PRESS

©2015 Milan Jesih \ Translation copyright ©2015 Nada Grošelj
Foreword copyright ©2015 David Bandelj
First edition, 2015 \ All rights reserved

LIBRARY OF CONGRESS CATALOGING-IN-PUBLICATION DATA

Jesih, Milan.
    [Poems. Selections. English]
    Selected poems / by Milan Jesih ; translated by Nada Grošelj. -- First edition.
        pages cm
    "Foreword copyright ©2015 David Bandelj" -- Verso title page.
    Includes bibliographical references.
    Summary: "A postmodern poet who successfully employed classic structures to
exploit the range of possibilities inherent in the Slovenian language, this selec-
tion from the life's work of Milan Jesih highlights his revolutionary approach
to verse. Beginning with humor and autobiography and gradually withdrawing
into a universe of fragments, quotations, dreams, and doubt, this collection offers
English readers a first glimpse into the work of one of Slovenia's literary treasures"
-- Provided by publisher.
    ISBN 978-1-62897-109-5 (pbk. : alk. paper)
    1. Jesih, Milan--Translations into English. I. Grošelj, Nada, translator. II.
Bandelj, David, writer of foreword. III. Title.
    PG1919.2.E77A2 2015
    891.8'415--dc23

                                    2015014830

This book is partially funded by a grant by the Illinois Arts Council, a state agency.
Published in cooperation with the Slovene Writers' Association—Litterae Slovenicae Series.

This work has been published with the support of the Trubar Foundation, located
at the Slovene Writers' Association, Ljubljana, Slovenia. This translation has been
financially supported by the Slovenian Book Agency.
With the support of the Creative Europe programme of the European Union.

This project has been funded with support from the European Commission.
This publication [communication] reflects the views only of the author, and the
Commission cannot be held responsible for any use which may be
made of the information contained therein.

www.dalkeyarchive.com
Victoria, TX / London / Dublin

Cover by Arnold Kotra

Typesetting: Mikhail Iliatov

Printed on permanent/durable and acid-free paper

Contents

The Mystery of the Subject vii
FOREWORD BY DAVID BANDELJ

The Mystery of the Subject

FOREWORD BY DAVID BANDELJ

A brief history of verse

Traditional Slovenian literary criticism has always associated the name Milan Jesih with the phrase *poetic modernism.* Viewed strictly from the perspective of literary science, this claim is justified, for Jesih's first poetry collection, *Uranium in the Urine, Master! (Uran v urinu, gospodar!,* 1972) continues the *apparent* ludism of Tomaž Šalamun. "Apparent" because ludism was not the artistic *credo* of the so-called modernists but merely a formal basis enabling the mimicry of the subject, a feature which was to become highly personalized in Jesih's writing. The history of Jesih's verse in fact spans a remarkable evolution or, in the words of Matevž Kos,[1] a sequence of poetic metamorphoses.

Janko Kos[2] suggested that Jesih belonged to the same generation as, for example, Ivo Svetina, but to a different type of poetry. According to Kos, Jesih's starting point is "poetic playfulness," and his collections show a largely modernist orientation toward an alogical flow of surprising associations and phrases: a flow which at the same time draws on a parody of the poetic tradition.

Jesih's second collection, *Legends (Legende,* 1974), already manifests an elaboration on modernist techniques and thus assumes a transitional role: the line gains in length and narrativity, thus paving the way for the twin summits of Jesih's

---

1 Matevž Kos: "Sonet kot forma prebolevanja vsakdanjosti." [The Sonnet as a Form of Recovering from Daily Routine.] *Fragmenti o celoti.* Ljubljana: LUD Literatura (Novi Pristopi Series), 2007. 153–169.

2 Janko Kos: *Pregled slovenskega slovstva.* [A Survey of Slovenian Literature.] Ljubljana: DZS, 1992. 377–378.

modernism, the collections *Cobalt* (*Kobalt*, 1976) and *Tungsten* (*Volfram*, 1980). With these, Jesih's energetic modernism peters out, and five years later his poetic composition is transformed in the collection *Lips* (*Usta*, 1985). If the subject of the first two collections invites identification with the author, the subject of *Lips* shakes off all subjective categories, searching for his place in pure poetry. In addition, the line of verse shortens: Matevž Kos[3] considers *Lips* a collection of poetic miniatures.

The peak of Jesih's writing, according to traditional literary criticism, occurs in the 1990s, which saw the publication of his *Sonnets* (*Soneti*, 1989) and *Sonnets the Second* (*Soneti drugi*, 1993). The regularity of their form and their connection to the France Prešeren tradition make Jesih a postmodernist who has successfully employed classic structures to exploit the range of possibilities inherent in the Slovenian language. The two sonnet books became popular and were widely read, perhaps partly due to the tradition of the Prešeren sonnet, which had been elegantly transplanted to the present in Jesih's approach. One of Jesih's distinctive features, according to Boris Paternu,[4] is that his poetry is not self-sufficient; rather, he is fully open to looking back, to the national poetic tradition, even to its best known and most brilliant classics. It is this tradition that he alludes to and blends into an innovative configuration. The same association continues in *Iambics* (*Jambi*, 2000), but this apparent structural rigidity in fact charges his language with even more meaning, which is why Jesih is considered a master of language in Slovenian poetry.

3 Op. cit.
4 Boris Paternu: "Jesih v klasiki." [Jesih among the Classics.] *Od ekspresionizma do postmoderne.* Ljubljana: Slovenska matica, 1999. 204–216.

Two subsequent anthologies, *Verses* (*Verzi*, 2002) and *Poems* (*Pesmi*, 2006), were followed in 2007 by the collection *So to Say* (*Tako rekoč*). *So to Say* inaugurates a type of composition which seeks, less gravely and with great harmony and elegance, a narrative mode—a mode which makes poetry a pure delight.

Continuing the trend of *So to Say*, the collection *Hundredtown* (*Mesto sto*, 2007), slightly more provocative but just as ironic, sets to verse the details of an imaginary town and its (petit) bourgeois life. And the latest collection, *Couldbe* (*Lahkoda*, 2013), is an elaboration of the poet's search for and omission of the subject in various tones, ranging from more to less serious. What preponderates is again a polished verse form.

This brief sketch is the history of Jesih's poetry as seen by mainstream Slovenian literary criticism. A minute examination of details, however, yields still another image of the poet and his work.

The subject: all or nothing

For the attentive reader, the most striking feature of Milan Jesih's poetry is the gradual withdrawal of the subject. Rather than a diachronic development from one collection to another, this is a result of the author's intention ever since *Cobalt*. If the subject of his debut collection, *Uranium in the Urine, Master!*, is heavily involved in daring and subversive poetic utterances, which literally "hit" the reader with their apparent playfulness, the subject of *Legends* takes to hiding in visionary and oneiric images. At this point we may stop to examine the *ludism* label attached to Jesih's poems, which can hardly be read as a mere toying with poetry. Certainly, Peter Kolšek's[5] afterword to Jesih's *Verses* remarks on the larger meaning of ludism: it is a daring, at times traumatic, counter-ideological campaign which breaks down both old ramparts and new barricades. This is certainly a more appropriate portrayal of the Slovenian ludism of the late 1960s and early 1970s. Yet Jesih's ludist phase soon peters out, and the *novum* of the two subsequent collections, *Cobalt* and *Tungsten*, is that they embark on the annihilation of the subject—a futile task because the poet himself admits[6] that the subject is not so easily annihilated: "Of course it's fine with me that my poem is not told from my own viewpoint, but it's not enough, I want it to be told from nobody's viewpoint. If it could be done."

The collections *Cobalt* and *Tungsten* bear eloquent titles: both refer to metals which are at once harder than iron and very brittle. Similar features mark the two collections. Both were printed in landscape orientation because the lines of verse became progressively longer. This extension brings, of course, an abundance of material which poses a challenge to the reader. On the other hand, the intrusion of "sentiment and melancholy"[7] speaks against a total adherence to modernist ideology which is eager to break from the past. In fact, Jesih's quest leans toward absorbing the past in his own poetry and recasting it with means of expression more suitable to this day and age.

Cobalt segues into a discourse on the art of poetry, on the

---

5 Peter Kolšek: "Podobar in podoba." [The Painter and the Painting.] Milan Jesih: *Verzi*. Ljubljana: Mladinska knjiga (Knjižnica Kondor), 2001. 203–226.

6 Tina Kozin: "Tri besede (Milan Jesih, intervju)." [Three Words (Milan Jesih: an interview).] *Literatura* XXIV / 247–248, January–February 2012. 88–102.

7 Matevž Kos, op. cit.

creation of worlds through poetry, on the truth or fictionality of poetic utterances. The poet (or his subject) seems to have reached a phase when he is intensely questioning his activity. Poetry turns into a string of images embedded in the safety of the verse, but the latter has no authority because the poet is continually testing its endurance. The images which superficially smack of modernism subtly express the predicament of the poem which tries to become the pure reflection of its self.

The ruminating quest continues throughout the collection, and certain flashes suggest that not all that glitters is gold—or to paraphrase . . . not all that is brittle is cobalt. Jesih's quest for expression is firmly rooted in the past; he seeks to give these roots a contemporary appearance, to sever the poem from himself, but this venture is by no means a facile or simple one. Rather, it springs from carefully considered choices, from his creative *métier* and bold decisions. If his *Cobalt* of 1976 claims: "It's not true that I call things by false names" and thus avoids fictionality at all costs, a more recent interview states: "[. . .] the poem is always smarter than the writer. There may come along a fine opening line in the first person, and then it's up to you to struggle with it."[8]

Thus Jesih is revealed as an author who in *Cobalt* embarked on an earnest search for the truth about himself, the world, and the act of creation. Nearly forty years later he realized that poetry was essentially the result of carefully considered choices. But the road that led to this insight enabled him to renounce the subject (at least in principle): the subject who, in Slovenian poetry, by definition both suffers and enjoys the fruits of his suffering.

8 Tina Kozin, op. cit.

The subject who is dead serious but converted by Jesih into an ironic *flâneur,* drifting through society. The subject who is capable of saying in the first phase of his quest: "What is said to you by the unknown in an unknown tongue is said to me by the known in a known tongue," thus setting a boundary for his quest. The subject's tongue turns and twists until another collection emerges, *Tungsten.* Here the subject's gradual *alienation* progresses in harmony with the preceding collection. Jesih begins by writing: "I am not I, I am a knife, I am a whip, I am a cry, I am rice, the water of silence, thick, imperturbable, I am the way and the sweat of the way." This entails renunciation of the poetic *persona* in the interest of the language and the images created in it. The effect becomes more varied and frequent in *Tungsten.* But among the lines we may find occasional orientation markers for the reader (and perhaps author), showing the path they are currently treading. Thus Jesih sometimes returns to the issue of selfhood in poetry:

> *The chasm of sky, beneath it, above it, a man's —*
> *my — thin silhouette; on my way to myself? Oh.*
> *   […]*
> *Halfway up the slope I stop, halting in midthought.*
> *Knowing? Seeking? On my way to myself? Oh.*

Such formulations make Jesih's poetry a modern (or — according to literary criticism — modernist) reflection on his current activity. The "right way" of poetry and the (il)legitimacy of the subject in this approach are no longer an issue; what emerges is a natural progression of events which reflect the state of the writing subject. An important issue is mastery over what has been written, a feature prominent in both—closely related—collections. The road to poetry's independence is a long one, and the author is aware of it. He jots down the images almost automatically, within the frames of a form which adapts itself to these images. These running notes are accompanied by occasional self-reflections which define poetry in *Cobalt* and *Tungsten* as a long meditation on poetics. A surprising kind of autopoetics. A reflection on what has been created—or, better yet, awakened.

Jesih's two "metal" collections are thus simply a road leading to the future through the past: a past which the author strives to leave behind but which increasingly becomes entwined in his text. This is achieved not only through numerous references but, above all, through the atmosphere evoked by a string of images, which are sometimes tinged with expressionism and imbued with a sense of the tragic.

Yet *Cobalt* and *Tungsten* were not enough. The ocean of verse lines (the longest lines in the history of Slovenian poetry, according to Peter Kolšek)[9] is fragile for all its solidity; to achieve a subjectless utterance would require lips speaking on their own. This image comes in handy in the next collection with a telling title: *Lips*.

After the arduous quest of *Cobalt* and *Tungsten*, the poet reappears with a considerably shorter verse form, renounces the first-person subject, and definitively ends his phase of extreme linguistic exuberance by adopting simple, almost rudimentary language material.

9 Peter Kolšek, op. cit.

Henceforth the poetry speaks for itself as Jesih retreats. The poet is only detected in the ingenuity of miniature flashes which are born of relativity, or in his masterful play with language. The withdrawal of the first-person subject is important not just because poetry thus meets irony, but also because the poet strips the long verse line, laden with meaning, of those elements which are related to the subject and therefore redundant. The meaning remains, as do certain reflections that touch on his timeless poetological theme. Some poems are thus subjectless but still clearly express their writer's intention:

> *How do poets write*
> *when they turn blue:*
> *with needlelike letters*
> *they touch*
>
> *the sky*
> *till blood comes*

In addition to the line shortening and the (at least apparent) absence of the subject, a distinctive feature of *Lips* is the enhanced polyphony of Jesih's idiom. *Lips* is an intermediary stop where the train of Jesih's creativity pulls up to reflect on its way forward. It is no coincidence that the book comes just before *Sonnets*, the collection which crystallizes Jesih's poetic idiom, for it is only by attaining his shortest possible verse form that he can move on, step onto the path of the defined iambic meter which finally establishes him as a full-fledged poet. *Lips* concludes with a well-founded doubt as to what may come next:

A slip of a verse
is crossing the field,
leaving a still
track in the grass.

Will anyone follow it here, so far,
with what hope?

This question is not addressed to the audience but to the poet himself. And the answer will only emerge four years later, in *Sonnets,* followed by *Sonnets the Second.*

With this, the subject disappears for good. Henceforth Jesih's poetry speaks for itself; the sonnet is chosen because of its link to the past—not merely the historical but the creative past. Here begins Jesih's language metamorphosis, which emerges out of tradition and returns to it, having sought on all previous forays the kind of poetic realization that would prove most suitable or our time. Instead of a *subject*, the floor is taken by a *speaker*.

Sonnets, a chapter unto itself

Although they are an integral part of Jesih's process of withdrawal, his sonnets require a separate chapter because it is here that his idiom, form, and maturity of content become fully established. Both of his sonnet collections have been minutely examined by literary scholarship and given favorable reviews, reviews testifying to their role not only in the author's personal development as a poet but in the context of Slovenian poetry as a whole. To cite some examples: Denis Poniž[10] concisely notes that Jesih's sonnets, which give voice to the poet's "journey" through real and imagined landscapes, contain an uncommon wealth of words, brightly colored contrasts, metaphorical turns, allusions to other poets, a postmodern blend of the most diverse impressions, perceptions, and visions. The phrase "the sonnet as a form of recovering from modernity" coined by Matevž Kos[11] clearly establishes that Jesih's sonnets approach the postmodernist experience of poetry and its tradition.

It was precisely characterizations such as these that led to the perception of Jesih's sonnets as postmodernist attempts to verbalize the world. True, in the late 1980s and early 1990s *Sonnets* certainly displayed an evident *zeitgeist* power, fusing with the postmodernist "model" which had emerged in Slovenian literary scholarship. But of equal importance is the autonomy of the author who has gathered in his sonnets the prestigious tradition of this verse form. The Slovenian sonnet blossomed with Prešeren and went on to be adopted by a number of Slovenian poets (even recent ones), who sought either to create their own versions of it or to adopt it as a classic form, a reference to the past, in their desire to establish artistic continuity and poetic excellence. Jesih's contribution to the sonnets centers on content rather than form. His form is impeccable, of course, but the real shift happens at the inner, subject-matter level: the confessions of the subject, who has been sought (or rather lost) in the previous collections, are transformed into the narrative

---

10 Denis Poniž: "1990–2000." *Beseda se vzdiguje v dim. Stoletje slovenske lirike 1900–2000.* [The Word Rises Up in Smoke: A Century of Slovenian Lyric Poetry 1900–2000.] Ljubljana: Cankarjeva založba, 2002. 269–281.

11 Op. cit.

of a voice which creates and renews landscapes from the past. To this end Jesih employs quotations as well, but without an artificial or constrained effect; they result from his poetic practice, an ecstatic flood of words that takes a different shape for each poet. Of his alleged postmodernism and the use of quotations associated with it, Jesih says:

> [W]ords like to flock together: once I've ferreted out the first ones, the rest will come of their own accord; I fire a signal rocket to call together the more desirable ones, with the right hair colors and finer measurements and a scandalous past and all their wear and tear and all that defines them, and then they parade on the catwalk like models and body-builders while I choose or reject them [...]. At first I was a bit wary of quotations but adopted them all the same; when I read how typical they were of postmodernism, something I must have overlooked before, I began to reject them but then accepted them again, thinking There's no harm in that, if they want me to be a postmodernist I'll settle for it, what the hell, the poem won't be any better or worse for it.[12]

Jesih's speaker is a narrator and painter. A narrator because the sonnets are largely characterized by discourse that is descriptive and unhurriedly rhythmical, presenting a landscape of words which coalesces into an image. But he is a visual artist as well (Kolšek[13] calls him a "painter" after one of his poems, "The painter and the painting") for the sonnets display a vivid visual

---

12 Tina Kozin, op. cit.
13 Op. cit.

element in their choice of metaphors. Far from being hermetic, these are clear and open, conjuring up an ambience which is interpreted by literary criticism as postmodernist. This quality, however, stems from the poet himself rather than from post-modernism. The setting, the chronotope to which the sonnets are attuned, is a fictional, remote, or not-so-remote past where the action, transplanted to the level of conceptions, slows down. Facts are no longer facts even if they appear as such. They are simply a way of expression which annuls the present and past, entering the *kairos* of poetry.

The imaginary landscape, and thus the imaginary *chronos*-turned-*kairos*, smoothly blends in Jesih's sonnets with the elements described by Boris Paternu[14] as the thematic circles of Jesih's poetry: existential, erotic, and poetological themes.

Despite the speaker in whom we encounter Jesih's "double," *Sonnets* is a brilliant opportunity for Jesih's personal voice to infiltrate his utterances, as it has done in *Lips*. This is performed with quiet elegance. The problems of employing the sonnet in this guise are introduced in the very opening line: "I'm not sure I can utter it at all." Later the subject's — yes, this time there is a subject!—difficulty in expressing himself is touched on in passing: "I haven't faced myself alone and nude." Or he may express his doubt in the *kairos*, which is spatial as well as temporal:

> *the world is, I am not: I'm one who lives*
> *caught between yes and no, distant from it.*

14 Op. cit.

Still other statements may be read as self-disciplining attempts to grasp the poetic materials—statements directing us to the "I" who is the true *subject*, the subject whom Jesih continually attempts to lose but can never fully shake off:

> *let me be me: sit small inside the house*
> *surrounded just by bare necessities.*

Or elsewhere:

> *I bloom and belch and shift into reverse;*
> *what is, is me; whatever lives, I live.*

Another defining feature of Jesih's sonnets is their variety of language, a polyphonic style that mixes higher and lower registers, Petrarchan verses and slang expressions. The sonnet experiment succeeded (even apart from the fact that *Sonnets* had two reprints) because the poet was able to revolutionize tradition and include it in the contemporary perception of the world, creating a book or, rather, two books which define a major leap in Slovenian poetry from tradition to the present with great artistic sensibility. Therefore Jesih's form is no superficial appearance or escape but a consistent choice which opens up the language in all directions. Even free verse, after all, can be perceived as a kind of formal choice. *Sonnets* evidently laid out for Jesih the setting of a poetic landscape which he was to continue in his iambics.

Where do we go from here . . .

In its essence *Iambics* is a collection of modified sonnets, for the poet has given up tercets in order to form poems of four, five, or six quatrains at most (with an occasional sonnet still thrown in) and thus continue down the path taken by the preceding two collections, equipped with a formal feature which will accompany him throughout the years. The mood of the *kairos* from *Sonnets* grows more intimate in *Iambics*. The frequent sonnet metaphors suggesting involvement in public life are reduced, giving way to the theme of being, of existence, which is underlined in most poems. Surprisingly, *Iambics* is hardly embedded in town life at all: there is instead a lot of nature, conjuring up a background of silence which accompanies the observations of Jesih's speaker. These are essentially bitter, melancholy, at times even tragic. It is possible to associate the existential mood radiating from the iambics (or *Iambics*) with the creation of a poetic mood: a mood which might link the world of imaginary facts, such as is found in *Sonnets*, to the world of imaginary emotions. This mood establishes the conditions under which the fictional image of a poetic world, a world such as is articulated by Jesih's speaker, can exist. In *Iambics*, too, some poems are imbued with the poet's spirit, especially those enclosed in parentheses. Some of them explain why the author chooses to create the image of a world which exists only in his thoughts, ideas, dreams:

> *([. . .] the sweetness of the blooming linden trees*
> *does not pass on because I keep it up,*
> *with choking breath and a suppressed heartbeat.)*

Yet this ethereal, fragile atmosphere is shattered in the next collection, *So to Say*, in its very first lines:

> *What I have sharpened still keeps slipping, vague,*
> *away from me, and seeps into oblivion.*

We are back at the drawing board. Jesih's intentional loss of the subject must continue. The speaker may stay, but the subject must disappear. The parenthesis represented by *Iambics* in the poetic circle of Jesih's writing closes and the subject is sent back into his imposed exile. It is as if the poems sought to awaken a momentary nostalgia for the subject and to test whether the acknowledged and established speaker of *Sonnets* might not at least "impersonate" the latter. The collection *So to Say* again delights in the joy of narrating and the flood of images, which sometimes masterfully interweave with the author's erudition and (reading) experience:

> *A second-hand bookshop: last night I leafed*
> *through reproductions of some painters' works:*
> *in an Impressionist paysage emerged*
> *a soldier — tiny, only just perceived . . .*

But hidden clues can be discerned to prove that the text has not been stranded — *so to say* — left without the author's signature. This becomes evident in the following poem:

> *The poet's old, and weakness is a daze;*
> *his hold has loosened and he now assents*

that things are alien to their names
because the names have turned to things themselves;

no longer luscious beauties of the south,
the poems are mere skeletons, mere frames,
he stammers clichés, cries without a sound
— he who could always sing to please the taste —

into a shifting glimpse of trembling lines,
into a maze of interrogatives;
what death has pre-elected is his mind
            — and yet the more his wisdom lives,

a wisdom that does not build verse, that's true,
but still lights up the building work itself —
No shape, no clay, a wire hacked to shreds,
he hovers in the final customs booth.

In addition to a pronounced (self) irony, the poem presents the author's reflection on his own work, a reflection ever wavering between despair and joy. In short, Jesih often portrays himself as a keen thinker on technopoetics.

The true twist in the collection, however, comes in its final section where Jesih's speaker confronts one of the themes most frequently addressed in poetry, death. Seemingly lighthearted, this confrontation actually deals with the fear which pervades all living creatures. Yet the poems are surprisingly bright even when they express finiteness, and especially once they have been stripped of the metaphysical nihilism which the poet (or his speaker) has been skeptical of ever since *Sonnets*. A playful treatment of the death theme occurs, for example, in the following poem from *Sonnets*:

> *And yet—again that "yet!"—if up should creep*
> *the Never-Asking White and ask of me*
> *if I was ready: "Coming, ball of grease?"*
>
> *"The road is broad, the boss has sent a jeep,"*
> *I'd answer: "Not right now . . . And, a propos,*
> *you needn't fetch me: I can walk alone."*

The narrative encountered in these poems thus fuses with a major subject-matter of Jesih's poetry, one which recurs in all of his collections. As passion and the tragedy of existence intertwine in many and varied forms, these two themes may be viewed as genuine companions of Jesih's work. The doubt about any kind of existence and the quest related to this doubt define the poet as a great seeker of purpose (or Purpose), who is aware that such a search may well lead to tragic ends, such as the void of nothingness. However, Jesih's doubt is not skeptical but Cartesian, the kind that may shed some light on existence.

These poetic voices, too, reveal the apparent absence of the subject, but the latter keeps intruding—at the very least through the author's choice of themes.

Thus it comes as a surprise that the collection *Hundredtown* continues the journey without a first-person subject, and that its speaker is a pure narrator. Again it is the town, growing into a large metaphor, which is foregrounded as the chronotope of action. Under a guise of irony, shallow routine and lack of sentimentality, this poetry cuts to the very core of man's purpose in the world.

The poetry again takes place in the *kairos*, renewing Wittgenstein's covenant to keep the essentials concealed. But in talking about marginal things, Jesih (or his speaker) in fact puts his finger on the primary goal of poetry—revelation:

> *A stone in town, what does it do?*
> *Squats—in the middle of the square, legs crossed—*
> *alone, defiant, brazen, never moved,*
> *as if to say: I challenge all your lot.*

The stone metaphor is appropriately used in this context to outline the poet's position in the surrounding world. The collection *Hundredtown* thus reinforces Jesih's role as a builder of worlds and images which define the present in a quasi-realistic manner. Prešeren's eternal dilemma between fear and hope is addressed through a fluctuating poetry which skillfully swings from one existential extreme to the other.

A close encounter with the purpose and "hope" of existence as perceived by Jesih's speaker calls attention to the theme of love. While this theme reaches its apogee in *Sonnets*, it occurs in the earlier and later poems as well, although with slight differences. If the pre-sonnet poems talk about love only indirectly, the sonnets are deeply stamped with surrender to the overwhelming force of love's eternal flame, but this is done in a *hopeful and narrative* manner rather than a *romantic and confessional* one.

The doubt about existence, or the *fear* of it, is redeemed by the *hope* of amorous encounters which bring meaning to the speaker's—and perhaps the poet's—world:

> *(if I should doze, o kindly God, then let*
> *a stranger in a blameless instant find*
> *that she has raced to meet me in her mind*
> *and let me dream of her with arms outspread)*

The aspect of time dissolves: the *kairos* of this poetry is the present, the *hic et nunc* moment of erotic ecstasy:

> *[. . .]*
> *two making love in steaming undergrowth.*
> *A kiss that, being eaten, does not bite;*
> *a clasp that squeezes but does never choke;*
> *a night-time meal without a board or knife!*
>
> *Above them lightly stirs a rustling leaf,*
> *the breeze comes licking sweaty, hot skin dry,*
> *the time is limpid, clear beyond belief,*
>
> *it is Forever which is called Tonight,*
> *ubiquitous yet present only there:*
> *beside the tranquil lake, some time, somewhere.*

Time, a category which is considered everlasting in love, narrows in Jesih's poems to a single moment. A fleeting moment, to be sure, but poetry seems created precisely for the purpose of arresting this moment, for dispelling any misgivings about the transience of love. In fact, time is love's strongest adversary:

> *I still remember tears and rants, the schnapps*
> *that I — the bloody idiot — went and gulped*
> *in that hotel room; sickness and disgust,*
> *the parting note that "she'd be sorry once"—*
>
> *and that is all; and all of it is veiled*
> *by fogs and vapors from the pulp I've read*
> *and half-baked films and fancies, dead as nails.*
> *No longer do those hours sear like death*
>
> *— those stumbling hours of searching for the cheat —*
> *instead they seem benign, like tourist rides:*
> *museums, parks, the Old Town dear to me,*
>
> *the fountain — how it gushed into the skies!*
> *How much of memory's power can remain*
> *when the first thing to melt down is the pain?*

The flight of time and transience of love are so closely entwined that they may be recognized as the leitmotif of Jesih's quest in erotic lyric poetry. Eroticism provides no real fulfilment: all that the theme seems to offer is the suggestion that the ecstasy of existence may yet be realized somewhere, but it is burdened with a gnawing doubt which hinders any optimistic view of the future. After *Sonnets*, the theme of love accordingly retreats into the background, resurfacing only at times as a bright, invigorating reminiscence which nevertheless leaves a deep doubt in its wake. In grappling with the greatest existential dilemmas, Jesih does not turn to love for support: he prefers to reflect on his work, seeking the purpose of the artist's activity.

On the other hand, a close look at the poems clustered around the poetological theme reveals a subtle form of self-redemption. Through his work, Jesih—or the poet/subject/speaker—merges into the structure of the universe and becomes part of the primordial plan which we shall never understand: the plan commonly referred to as fate, god or the like. The immeasurability of Jesih's address to god (or God), which ranges from irony and even sarcasm to deadly earnestness, reflects his multi-faceted confrontation with the world and its illogical logic, a confrontation which is, after all, the arch-origin of all outstanding literature. Therefore the verses meditating on creation are in fact verses written by a *creator*. Seen in this light, they merge with the ancient dictum that says poets create not merely poetry but the universe or world itself. As a poet, Milan Jesih, too, engages in creation to keep fear at bay and to foster hope, a prerequisite for any creative act. This is aptly summarized in the concluding poem of his first sonnet collection, a statement of the poet's urge to articulate and create, which is both natural and inscribed in the universe:

> *(I nibbled on my pen the livelong day*
> *and racked my brain for just one line of verse,*
> *as if I tried to chirrup down a bird*
> *to perch on my wide open palm and stay,*

and nothing still—but when I closed an eye
and nodded off, dejected, in my seat,
my doze drew unknown lines from outer dreams
—of Everything: of Beauty, Truth And Light—

they left me gawping, humbled, stricken low
before a force that slips the waking grasp,
for in the rose's name there grew a rose

and in the sound of "heart" there beat a heart . . .
Awake, I now recall no theme or word.
But such a sonnet is, somewhere on earth.)

It is impossible to sum up an oeuvre that is still in the making. There is no telling how Jesih may surprise us in the future. What is certain is that a poet of his ilk not only possesses an artist's sensibility but also demonstrates the magic of language which comes, goes, and oscillates, while the poet / creator's role is merely to shape it. Sometimes he does it by himself, but sometimes it is the language that does the shaping, the poet being a mere tool in its hands. The dividing line between them is a mystery which remains unknown.

TRANSLATED BY NADA GROŠELJ

Milan Jesih: Selected Poems

Lips (1985)

* * *

On the water glides
a wooden duck.
The summer fades.
From a grandchild, how

does a grandma sprout?
Just wait a while.

* * *

A slip of a verse
is crossing the field,
leaving a still
track in the grass.

Will anyone follow it here, so far,
with what hope?

* * *

In the sky, the wrap
of a silver gull—
who can pluck it down?

* * *

A milky morning
spills
over spilt
morning milk.

* * *

A tomcat wades straight
in the young snow and dusk,
sweetly you close your eyes
after him.

* * *

Short it has been,
the night,
the day has
stretched it a little.

Sonnets (1989)

* * *

At night there pressed a wind, a sudden dash,
the trees in blossom poised themselves to flee
from their orchard—but the thunder flashed
and froze them in a white and silent scene:

time thickened in an ill-foreboding threat
of pouring rains and gales and rising floods;
the bellies of the clumsy clouds were thrust
against the belfry; driven, black and set

against the black, they brought the bronze to moans—
you closed the window but you lingered near
"until the first rain droplet overflows";

you've snapped awake and opened it because
the moon is lit, the air is crisp and clear,
the nightingale is warbling on, still moist.

* * *

I think a scene: the east room; she and I,
curled up into a dot all soft and warm;
above the plain a vast and rising dawn;
she sleeps at peace, the green and quiet sky

comes gloaming in the home that ever preys;
with breath as slight as one who halfway died,
her lips are parted for a soundless cry,
she roams, in scattered sleep, the spacious gaols

of narrow distances, to passing doomed;
I think the handsome face grown finely lined
(long live the shameless pathos in which time

delights while moving down its secret path!) —
a fragile scene, an image in full bloom
that fattens in my breast, a thirsty bat.

* * *

The wind is chasing an old rag away.
Flocks gather in the sky for southern lands:
a flight of restless speckles, grey on grey.
You people walk in couples, holding hands,

and pass through autumn, quiet, with loving hearts,
like coming, sunk in thought, from services.
A fleeting dark and fiery sunset darts
to crimson up your ancient cobbled streets,

but just as night falls and beyond your sight
the distances are sensed as drawing near,
they spread — "Dear God, this hurts!" — a headless fright

and, quivering and fragrant, disappear.
And then arises, destined for all time,
the silence with its never-ending whine.

* * *

Hey, lambs are prancing in the snow, some white,
some black, while all around lies sleeping night,*
the wolf, the bell, the village; those who died
by fire and by water; time and tide;

asleep lie winter and the wind, the wood,
the brook and ice, the foot tracks in the snow,
the palfrey harnessed by a sleeping youth
before a sleeping sled at sleeping home

(asleep the cellar, rooftop, stony threshold);
asleep the stars, unspeakably remote,
the king beneath the hill, the hill, volcano

(the sleep-sunk magma tossing to and fro);
and lust and pleasure, slime and spit — and you
who count the lambs in sleep: sleep on, you too!

---

* *while all around lies sleeping night:* a reference to Joseph Brodsky's "Elegy for John Donne" (*Bolshaya elegiya Dzhonnu Donnu*), which inspired this poem. (Author's note.)

* * *

Like dreams: a star glints white at heavens' heart,
the wind is flowing, hushed, from valley beds—
uncertain spring has started on its path
in Eastern Alpine suburbs. Rousing dread,

a cherub flaps above the somber moor,
now knocking down a bat with massive quill,
now sticking rabbits with his she-wolf thought,
now fanning flames to make the dinner spill;

a birch may quiver or a stone may droop;
a giggle curls a little girl's tress;
the siren of an ambulance may hoot;

by water's edge a wakeful village rests.
The mighty mindless angel flies and flies,
a sacred brute— no memory, lust or eyes.

* * *

A lover stands, a letter never sent,
beside the water of the shady eve;
beside the fishpond in its misty wreath
where Venus seems a wound, in heavens cleaved,

exposed to light; uncombed, he has been packed
off to the edges of a bland paysage;
the dead watch stands, will not be bribed aside
when nothing's left of flags but tattered scrap

and all his inward struggles have been lost;
he's stopped, without a movement or grimace
or looks, as if he'd frozen in his pace

beside that surface, never creased or crossed;
the beast of silence, grazing high in space,
now bellows over him in untamed lust.

* * *

A stone there is that ever struggles up
to lie back in its puddle, glimpse the skies,
but blindness brought by mud will not subside
and gravity, once well within its grasp,

has lost its bearings through the centuries;
the stone is man, who, blade of grass in hand,
is blending down the road of dirt and sand
into still shadows of the oozing eve;

the stone is song, heard scattered in the wind
when he has stopped before a village door,
and stony man, his pluck kept up no more,

is nodding: "Sweet wife, is it you who sing?"
—when it has, thawed to silence, taken wing
to soar among the new stars evermore.

* * *

Tonight is time a glove, its warmth not lost,
laid carefully upon a bed of sedge;
the west horizon has a wiry edge
of sunset, yellow from the golden bronze;

before me lies an epic Russian tale,
a tome set on the plains of sodden North,
and all that I have garnered on this day
and all that has been stored in memory's vault—

but what is real? October country night?
A mellow alto on the radio?
The lonely fasting of my lovestruck plight?

The wars and riots far off, long ago?
It all exists and yet eludes pursuit:
each scene is topped and ousted by a new.

* * *

How plain and simple! Birds are chirping, leas
are waving in the early summer breath,
an ant is smuggling home a night moth — dead,
the clinking bell is calling home from fields.

It's Now: the only time that lives its fill,
so fleeting that it cannot reach an end.
The thief has hid his booty in his den,
the bronze has slammed its portholes, throbbing still,

fresh force is being mustered by the breeze.
How plain and simple! "Now" is evermore,
the mighty Now holds time in viselike squeeze,

and so the moth shall live eternally,
the bell shall wait for one to ring its ore,
the country air shall glance around the fields.

* * *

A day, a meadow bright with marigolds,
where, taken by the hand, a couple comes
and, like the day, so pass all days and months;
alive with flowers, it is decked by snows;

as they love now, so their ways shall split,
unravel shall the fingers, closely wound,
and rot the blossoms, offered to the ground.
Yet somebody shall roam those forests still,

and who can say but one day he may see
the pair—in May, when Sunday has arrived
and one drives off into the countryside:

they shall be walking on the golden green,
both drunk on such sweet-blooded dreams again.
Again the years shall be one single day.

* * *

Damp is the evening, and the slimy clouds
are rubbing their bellies on the alp;
outside the inn, some migrants from the south
are singing sevdah songs, transfixing, dark.

At such a time I want to fall, to fall,
forget myself, to be the rain, to tear
and stab the stubbled fields, alive no more,
to draw thick hatches in the blunted air

till all things vanished from the face of earth
in watery yarns of pre-beginning sleep
and from foundations sprang another birth —

at first mere nothing, then a mist should seep,
and snow from milk — and in a dot, all light
condense together in majestic might.

* * *

I stare, each evening, how the moments flee.
From cider is October sweet, and gilt
where golden cider has on clouds been spilt,
and mellowed by a puppet, kind and sweet,

which here resides alone with me alone,
refusing to express itself in speech,
just staring at the ceiling from its seat.
A living woman's gift from long ago.

So race the days. And each new morning feels
like it was morning everlastingly;
come night (as now), however, it appears

that I have always lived a quiet eve—
precisely as one knows what lies ahead,
while for the past I wait with bated breath.

* * *

Some time, somewhere by water standing still
—a lake, most likely (and the moon's new arc
is late: until it rises, shall the dark
from darkness over into darkness spill)—

two making love in steaming undergrowth.
A kiss that, being eaten, does not bite;
a clasp that squeezes but does never choke;
a night-time meal without a board or knife!

Above them lightly stirs a rustling leaf,
the breeze comes licking sweaty, hot skin dry,
the time is limpid, clear beyond belief,

it is Forever which is called Tonight,
ubiquitous yet present only there:
beside the tranquil lake, some time, somewhere.

* * *

I still recall my autism as child:
I need but wink and all the world will cease,
a mise-en-scene meant only for my eyes.
I only have to open them to seize,

to spring upon that absence suddenly —
then I shall see, shall see . . . A little boy,
I toyed and toiled at this for many years
to glimpse the Nothing and confound its ploy.

But since I ripened and decay appeared,
I've worn spectacles of different hues:
I like to stroll along green strips of field,

at inns I'm shaken from a tipsy snooze,
I see that quondam scenery through and through,
and Nothing has been long left unconcealed.

* * *

I stood inside my space, inside my room,
as heavy as if absent, slightly dead
I probed my memories for greater depth;
meanwhile the city had been sunk in gloom.

I crossed toward the window, unaware;
a noise — a string has broken in the skies,
says Chekhov — soundless as the wind that dies;
and far away (so like the fiery glare

ablaze in snakeskin eyes that close to rest,
the image of a star in mica caught)
has something happened — in the grassy scents,

in sprays of water through some narrow gorge —
and burnt me through: a mighty new excess
of love without a body or address.

* * *

I look at landscape: at a narrow gorge,
a river, current-curling, green and cold,
which flows with eager lust to lengths untold;
above is untouched azure, heavens' vault.

Here let me pause, dear God, without a memory.
Forget that you have kneaded me a man
defined by dress and by his wristwatch brand,
and nail me, as a young stone, to the reef

with all the ruthless fury of your love! —
to hang above the water's rush and surge
(of stone is every blossom, fruit and seed)

in lands where freedom is a pressing urge,
to savor with a single sense the tough
and ever present mercy: just to be.

* * *

The hedgehog-hunting night has caught its game
and, crunching at its leisure, splits and splits
the lot in sudden, arrowshotlike pricks
that flood the body, spreading through each vein.

To close my eyes: let none of all the sights
I've seen — the trees in spring with blooming crowns,
the Children's Plague, the fires on the clouds —
let none appear again before my eyes.

And yet — again that "yet!" — if up should creep
the Never-Asking White and ask of me
if I was ready: "Coming, ball of grease?"

"The road is broad, the boss has sent a jeep,"
I'd answer: "Not right now . . . And, a propos,
you needn't fetch me: I can walk alone."

* * *

I'd like to visit Rome, but there's a town,
Odessa, calling with more primal force:
I must have vowed my mistress in the course
of one of my past lives to settle down

where she was born, and never stir from here:
but our ship was wrecked at Dardanelles
and she is wearing still her bridal veils,
a white old woman waiting on the pier.

Now let me cup her withered head at last
and kiss the toothless lips: before the eye
of God we two are one. And let us clasp

each other tight while gazing eagerly
at flocks of fishing boats afloat at night
against the murky hint of sky and sea.

* * *

A dream recalled? A memory dreamed up?
A sluggish river, nightingales. And low
inside my head crescendos an unknown
and far-off voice, grown dark with heavy lust,

to dupe me with a trick, a phantom formed
from fireflies: there glides, barefoot and bright
against the dusk, the girl whom I've adored
throughout my life: she floats with steps so light,

with skirt cascading deep but always dry
(and how the son of wind does make it reel!),
outgracing every grace; she comes indeed,

a flower in her hand, a glowing eye,
which I can make out well, besides her smile—
a dream remembered, dreamed-up memory.

* * *

The evening trains — the windows all aglow
and racing out to distant wonderland:
sometimes I was allowed to gawp and stand
if Mum was in the mood to take a stroll

at dusk with me along the iron bars:
a booming engine spitting sparks and soot,
with smell of brimstone trailing in pursuit
to fade away in magic foreign parts.

Then, after many years, those evening trains,
eyed by us soldiers with a wistful gaze,
would hammer on and on of home, sweet home.

Now there are none. Of course they still pass by
— that's not the question (neither the reply) —
but where should I at nightfall long to go?

* * *

If chance comes up again, o Father mine,
I beg you to create me as the snow.
Just strew me over wintry tundra, low,
and let me with my thousand eyes be blind,

so I may not divine a distant South:
without a memory, smell, or taste, or will
perfect me, God: just silence lying still
and crystals — stabby, motionless — inside.

I'm too confused by halfness of the whole,
and wholeness of the half, in human form,
so hear me, God of Justice: make it so

that I need never struggle any more
among the pell-mell promises and threats
to seek my fear and hope all by myself.

* * *

O lucky you, the man who zapped his father
when — tyrant that you are — you aimed a knock
right at the pate of Laius, the old crock;
and banged Jocasta, your own native mother,

on many sweaty nights till break of day
until that heavy royal bunk would shake —
you father-killing son, your mama's mate,
your children's brother, you are on your way.

You've had your share of bliss and now of grief.
You're bearing handsome gifts as broken, blind
on this fine payday you are leaving Thebes;

turned out of doors, you can be satisfied
that you've been well and ultimately screwed:
a bit alive but finished through and through.

* * *

I'd stand before the rifles, dressed in white,
while thinning mist should from the marshes creep:
the officer's curt order, almost shriek . . .
and hear no more the gunshots packed up tight,

in one great bang, to rouse the birds above
from living nests and make them flap about—
then I should dumbly scream the name of love,
prostrate, into the shrine of stars snuffed out . . .

and after many years of still-decay,
when bullets had been drunk in by the ground,
then from the heart a lonely reed should sprout,

spurred by an urge which, left without a coat,
is not a gift of memory but of hope,
the only heirloom of my living day.

* * *

The stairs of that old house which is the home
of one fine lass who holds me in her grasp
lead upward, all the way to dizzy stars
and on to lands unspeakably remote,

where every road and roadsign fades away
— where, cornered by the lyric genre rule,
the time I've had so far should be reduced
to form the prelude to a lover's tale.

But I won't let it. True, I sometimes creep
on those old stairs to slouch in coughy smoke,
I rip her stockings in a feverish sleep:

I want her so I feel that I must choke.
But if I gave in, I should lose my self:
and who should be the one who loves her then?

* * *

I still remember tears and rants, the schnapps
that I — the bloody idiot — went and gulped
in that hotel room; sickness and disgust,
the parting note that "she'd be sorry once" —

and that is all; and all of it is veiled
by fogs and vapors from the pulp I've read
and half-baked films and fancies, dead as nails.
No longer do those hours sear like death

— those stumbling hours of searching for the cheat —
instead they seem benign, like tourist rides:
museums, parks, the Old Town dear to me,

the fountain — how it gushed into the skies!
How much of memory's power can remain
when the first thing to melt down is the pain?

* * *

The time is wise with what is yet to come:
the children like two lambs, entwining close,
the night above them clear and bottomless,
nowhere does but the faintest echo plumb.

With force profound the taste of honey spills:
it beckons closer, promising to yield,
abundant where its depths are most concealed,
if only one surrenders first and wills;

more sweet and deadly still are ecstasies
when soul with a beloved soul entwines
and body tastes another body's lines:

then each into a shoulder sinks their teeth,
and each cries out, the only one to see
the other: "Nearest near, come nearer me!"

* * *

(I nibbled on my pen the livelong day
and racked my brain for just one line of verse,
as if I tried to chirrup down a bird
to perch on my wide open palm and stay,

and nothing still—but when I closed an eye
and nodded off, dejected, in my seat,
my doze drew unknown lines from outer dreams
—of Everything: of Beauty, Truth And Light—

they left me gawping, humbled, stricken low
before a force that slips the waking grasp,
for in the rose's name there grew a rose

and in the sound of "heart" there beat a heart . . .
Awake, I now recall no theme or word.
But such a sonnet *is*, somewhere on earth.)

Sonnets the Second (1993)

* * *

The Yuletide night is dry, with falling snow;
with mountains growing without cease or sound;
with folds of whiteness settling on the ground
to bring the springtime streams to overflow;

with mankind sleeping in forgotten dells;
with stars that hide in absence their blaze;
with glowing life within the earthy depths
that knows no paths to shallow nests of snakes.

A lonely God has slumped beneath the strain,
facing His son's birth, racked by nervous fears
as a director doubting his own play,

his mighty confidence now frayed and torn.
A radar silence that will not be pierced.
The whitening mountain dusk grows close to dawn.

* * *

An evening of unutterable hush,
not ruffled even once by noise or wind
or by the fitful fireflyish glint
among the valley pines by which I pass—

a stroller, there I saunter like a creel
sent floating down the river's sluggish flow,
a royal bastard: "How his eyes do gleam!"
might spit an ancient washerwoman: "Coals

of living fire—he must be an imp";
so there I saunter—seeming just to loaf,
but really steering for the village inn—

I saunter, an obscure and idle oaf,
a lukewarm dust now half returned to dust,
a dandelion clock held in my clutch.

* * *

Through every countless and inhuman day
I mooch around the world and find no rest;
in mellow moments when the sun has set
and when the night has chewed the evening's tail,

when in the moonless coldness may be felt
that mighty distance, opening away
to every side, unbounded and unstemmed,
it's then and always that I, restless, trail

along the streets: but sometimes I am stayed
and stilled inside myself, and when I stop,
it is, if I may call a spade a spade,

where Death is running his old knocking shop:
and there, my homey pipe in mouth, I stop
to stare at closed and curtained window slots.

* * *

A fenced-in backyard—tufts of meager weed,
woodsheds, a rotten Fiat without wheels—
a tenant strums, with intervals between
(in which he keeps his bottle's company);

and all lasts on and on; a dry wind stirs
and dies away; and there are no great themes:
the sixties, suburb of the capital,
late spring—or just a trick of memory?—

I was a child, and reading: dusk came on,
but I just sat as though I'd sighted time,
which ever plummets through the starry sky

and, overwhelming, carries all along . . .
And then, I like to think, the church bell struck
just when my mother called me in to sup.

* * *

Standing with all my might beneath the stars,
I lose myself in those dear olden days
when Mum would call to supper through the dark—
then all the world was simple, clear and straight,

the years were bursting up before my gaze,
years of a stormy, virile, fearless youth,
there was a mighty, still uncrumbling faith
and in my heart of hearts a great hope grew—

Now I know fear, and would not rather not;
for any faith I've lost I do not mourn;
what's alien in me feels strange no more;

I'm not ashamed of shallowness and rot.
But I like to revisit still at times
those days before I turn in for the night.

* * *

From Klagenfurt were broadcast chiming tunes,
my mum was rolling dumplings in her palms
and smiling lost in thought, so gentle, calm,
as I passed her the plums and sugar cubes;

and I remember other days — and chimes —
the foreign dishes and the dizzying
closeness of others — and their distances —
cocooned in memory I sail my life,

I live remembering. For hours on end,
sitting without a shadow, outline, weight,
unstirring, I can gaze at nothing's depth

while riding in the dawn of eastern plains.
Now I don't claim that both are true, because
true's neither. I'm remembering. That's all.

* * *

A gold and copper sunset in the dusk,
alone, is fading on the edge of day
on hilltops like a diadem of blood.
Beneath the boughs with their stir and sway

out in the garden, she and he partake
of love, a timeless, memoryless cup;
he — I — sits opposite and, face to face,
we're gazing our fill. The pleasure's cut

is both at once: a gash and scar closed up.
The wind that paused is once more on its way
across the garden, and his dampened train

brushes our faces lightly, without aim;
by instinct, for a blink, we close our eyes;
and here's the vast, immeasurable night.

* * *

The image of a woman's swaying hips
as she steps naked from the foam and brine
and, lustful, gasps for breath like netted fish
and blooms with pleasure, fades into decline;

as, almost out of mind, she stirs above
in topsy-turvy cries of passing flocks,
or stirs from window flowers fed by frosts
or from the scent of a caressed new love

—a knife, in slumber tempered, driven home.
You sense her, unknown, in your guts: a boy,
bewildered, it's for *her* you're beating off,

for her you never leave a girl alone,
for her you take a stranger for your wife,
for her you've lived and led a wretched life.

* * *

The mellow theater of budding night!
A genial wind is blowing from the lake:
and as it draws the curtain, airy-light,
it might be dancing with the moonshine ray

and with their shadows, too — two negatives —
receding further in the mirror's depth.
I know, and wait for her, the Undeceived,
to break with me the solitary bread

— as music never speaks to our kind
and yet again it does, with boundless grace,
so even disembodied love can thrive

and love will be most lovely once I'm dead —
then, sated with oblivion, we'll laugh
at life and all its forms of shallow lust.

* * *

Stirred by the wind, the book flipped to a page
and I believed I saw the phrase flash by:
"Dead, he loved her who had already died,"
but later I searched high and low in vain,

I chewed through all that portly cloying tome,
to grasp it in its context—whiled away
a day of life I'd scrimped and toiled to save.
Now, smiling at a sky of evening gold,

my memory, seeking memories, always finds
faces that are unknown but nest inside—
what are they?—corpses, faded, burnt to ash,

amazed how time had withered in a flash.
Whatever's past will be no more. From love
—the many and the one—I've sobered up.

* * *

When I was barely stirring in the dawn
— the laughter of young merry chimneysweeps
came neighing over city roofs and eaves —
and while there dawdled still about my straw

and warbled in my heart the happy hope
that all my early trials would console
and reassure me: "We were just a joke,"
and I was half-afloat above my doze —

who but the kind redeemer came to prick
me with her august call as with a pin,
to drive away the lies of milky dreams

and that I, guided by her stern decrees,
might press ahead and in the distant mists
raise up a stone and disappear beneath.

* * *

Two junipers have stopped in their tracks,
like brothers bringing up an ancient grief:
perhaps at odds which owned a stony stack,
which junipers will graze instead of sheep —

I watched a while, then turned among the trees
and sat down on a stump while all around
the chant of birds rang with a frenzied sound.
And not a single thought occurred to me

except for you know what: elated lines
which will not be expressed in words at all,
apostrophizing a — yet unknown — wife,

were blazing in my heart like bread of straw.
The wind curled like a dog beside my feet
to keep an iron loner company.

* * *

I've eaten well and will again tonight,
and meanwhile lord it in my garden: wallow,
strut valiantly, dally with the bottle,
and live, and roast inside my heart the ice

(if I should doze, o kindly God, then let
a stranger in a blameless instant find
that she has raced to meet me in her mind
and let me dream of her with arms outspread):

so pass my days. No trace remains behind:
as there is nothing left when I have hurled
a hullo at some bird that, passing by,

has swooped adventurously close to earth —
            The time bends down to lay
on me, unmoving, one more spade of clay.

* * *

All day I've lived. In early morning, first
I checked the writing of the day before
(reined in the pathos: passion's *p* is small)
and headed for the city's bustling stir,

saw pretty women in the market place,
bought some anchovies, washed them down at home,
and authored a small jar of marmalade;
I read and had a nap, alive I woke

and went on living. As the dusk drew close,
I did as planned: with time left to dispose,
I knotted round my neck an evening tie,

dabbed on some scent, and went to see a play.
The piece was dreary, drained of spice and life.
I had a Chardonnay. I've lived all day.

* * *

The autumn's come among the murky trees;
at times the wind in passing stops to pet,
offhandedly, a wolf's quick-witted head
and wades again into the knee-deep leaves.

In town, we men come crowding dingy bars,
unhappy, heavy, thirsty from the roads;
and oaths are our greetings, our toasts,
which bring no cheer to anybody's heart.

We gulp as many tears as drops of wine,
a sticky lump of grief goes with each glass:
it tastes of death, small-scale but sure to pass.

The stove, still cold, has raised a testy whine.
As for the wind: it halts, as has been said,
and bows to autumn at an idle length.

* * *

A scene that I had never seen, except
perhaps in dreams, upon an unknown time,
or that had washed up from a book I'd read
in younger days, and is now glorified

by tricky memory, faithful slave to hope:
the field is being ploughed, the horse's legs
sink hock-deep in the soil; along the road
are coming, nodding affably their heads

in greeting, wife and husband, faces still
aglow with smiles, their arms all but entwined.
Above them flits a *putto* — butterfly,

I see them greet the ploughmen. And the slit
cut into soil, grown newly aged, smells dark —
I'll pass away when this mirage has passed.

* * *

My gaze is bent on kindly olden times
—I liked to cheat my mum at dominoes
while looking straight in her beloved eyes;
the first school visit to a drama show;

the pics of naked ladies on the sly,
and on a Sunday, hoots of football freaks—
relentlessly alone I stand outside
and now is now, and all changed utterly.

It's autumn. Country fires have been lit
all over fields and weekend cottage plots.
The fire warms, the firewater burns

along the throat, the smoke makes nostrils sting.
A cloud of bloodied cotton floats aloft.
With tooth and nail I hold on to the world.

* * *

The village cottages are lighting up,
the prayer said, the quiet meal at end,
and as I saunter all alone through dusk
by willows on the facing river edge

and listen for the harps whose strings are played
by lovely daughters, spreading their thighs
so modestly; as, dragging on my pipe,
I blow the smoke to skies gone purple grey,

my heart is easy, for if God should call
on me to join Him in the muddied flow,
the cries and moans and fainting echoes all

should be shut out by windows lit with gold,
nor should the music falter in its sway
but go on floating, gentle, on the waves.

* * *

(Now, there are poems filled with poplar lanes,
with steeds of wind and their airy deaths,
with yellow-colored dandelion glades
through which a couple of young lovers treads;

and then realities, where shining trains
as quick as lightning whiz past semaphores,
like good old monsters from the fairy tales,
to spur the vivid fancy of young boys;

and there is, when you close your eyes, a hush
which sounds like an unmoving, dazzling glint:
it flashes from a memory bottled up

with the uncanny speed of hunting fish;
and there's a home in untold distances
where I will find my rest and sleep and sleep.)

Iambics (2000)

* * *

On one forgotten evening, long gone by
—it may have been the mellow time of spring
when no-one shuts the windows for the night
but wakens when the birds begin to sing—

on one forgotten evening, long gone by
—since then decades of years have come and passed
(but then: how can you ever measure time?)—
you came out of the house, to live at last:

the half-full moon has grown to half its round
—fresh weather comes, the almanac has said—
the sky might well be taking shape but now,
with swarms of stars caught fast in widespread nets,

the silence of the vast primeval realm,
opaque as yet, is creeping from the sides
into the seeming depths of firmament
—on one forgotten evening, long gone by—

you snap under your breath: "There's nothing new,
the tangy garden smell, the sanded walk,
nocturnal tracery above the roofs
—and the impatience of the missus' call—"

to dull the bursting zest that overran
on that forgotten evening, long gone by
— the soil awakened and the trees in sap —
your hungry heart for once and for all time.

* * *

In heaven's vault are carved the looming cliffs
and on the topmost cliff is perched a rock,
from it, a rockling lightly crumbles off,
an eaglet's droppings fall in the abyss;

there hover in the air lost vaulted halls
with dancing girls of hopes and memories
and wine is poured out freely, passing sweet,
and so the noon is gone and evening falls

and never does the image change a whit.
Now and again, an elf will squash a fruit
stashed in his pocket, stumbling over roots;
the rain may fill a hollow to the lip

and in may sometimes leap a startled frog;
come winter, winds come ripping leaves from boughs;
at times a wolf skull washes from the bog;
as it has ever been, so it is now.

* * *

A modest land: a shallow sinkhole tilled
and flanked by skimpy vine: an arid time
because the fish that bears us* has stopped still
in far-off absence, with a vacant eye

— now can you picture her?—the hotspur gust,
the wanton who will play through every prank,
who pauses, sweeping, in his very thrust,
has bolted from behind a crumbling shack

— now can you picture him?—and all has stopped
as if all untamed force had given in
before the karstlands' stubborn-headed whim:
observe those nettles, ashes, barren rock

and note the hands, locked resting on the ass,
the look that pierces the unmoving freeze,
the soil that's charged with wrath beneath your feet
and only wants to be, no more than that,

to be, unhindered by caprice or game:
and can you picture, wife, the sheer relief
when all that pent-up power is released
and twilight settles, calm as every day?

---

* *the fish that bears us:* reference to a gigantic mythological fish that was believed to carry
  the world on its back. (Translator's note.)

* * *

With each breath, autumn deepens by a stitch.
It deepens into void and the unknown:
the sunset copper frizzles the sun's disc,
you stare in childlike wonder, a man grown

—and all that ever was, in living hush,
comes flooding back as soon as eyes have closed:
no moment ever passes in its rush:
the tender yieldings, the betrayals low,

all go on in your heart, unmarred, unspoilt,
and have not through the years unlearnt to be—
your hands, created for the goodly toil,
rest clasped behind your ass, reflectively,

while through the reamers courses blood and time.
Over the fields descends a lonesome haze.
The manes of Mustangs, halted in the sky,
burst, one dry instant more, into a blaze.

* * *

A dirt road past a hayrack: haltingly
before a dung cart plods a nag away;
throughout the village pours the sunset's gleam
and pours the honey of the heavens' blaze;

inside a clock which, left unwound, has ceased,
a one-legged spider acts as engine jack;
time's standing still and learning just to be;
a draft leafs lightly through the almanac;

the dusty Christ has dozed; the Penates sleep;
the cat purrs on, a warm and compact ball
—a different theme are distances at sea,
a boy in white at gunpoint by the wall—

When Pegasus's kin glides down the roof,
the peace is shattered by the Ave bell,
the globe spins round again, well-oiled and smooth,
the image of an eve is all that's left.

* * *

Look how that juniper has spread its sails:
the top dog here, I guess. But bless my eye!
a year ago it still grazed rocks in gales,
and now it stands erect and steers our isle

—with all its seas and starlings, coves and doves,
the air and war and plasm and ore and boats,
the future tense, Jamaica, hunger, love,
the blindness, gnosis, firetongs, evils, woes—

and hums in that time-honored cone-tree way
(a soundless forte in the distant roots)
a breezy couplet on the passing day
and takes from "Lieber Augustin" its tune—

Can you, too, sense the winter drifting sweet
between the parted lips of waning day?
Let's tiptoe past, my wife, on soundless feet.
Give me your hand and let us steal—this way.

* * *

There is a garden; and outside its fence
a day like other wilting autumn days:
a day steeped in the silent country scents
of fires faded or about to fade;

there is a garden, dummy, fake and glum,
as if a demiurge should play, a child,
and drop his game, distractedly begun,
down on the ground like, say, a buttered slice:

a man is standing in the garden's heart,
left incomplete by what has been withheld;
a game which, unaborted, lost its path,
a bitter autumn's day, as I have said;

and there's a cry, a dry and silent wheeze
arising from a breast left half unfilled,
and even when the unplayed day has dimmed,
the cry remains and roams across singed fields.

* * *

A glass unemptied, half a bite of bread,
and all snuffed out. The hollow morning gleam:
locked in embrace, a sleeper and his dream
—or is it pillows, tangled in a spread?—

the air, uncertain, in the curtain stirs
before the window . . . with its squinting gaze
to far horizons . . . young and stormy days
. . . a lane and poplars and the city's verge

and—no, not really . . . Maybe on a cliff
an eagle has just spread his wings to soar . . .
The unknown mirrors in the river's glint
—an unknown weakness as an unknown force—

just for a glimpse, and then again dissolves
back into the no-night no-day—
Two clinging, moaning pillows, both absorbed—
as he in hers, so she in his, embrace.

* * *

It is a Sunday at the break of spring
and windborne thoughts are woven into time;
all those who love are quietly wandering,
held by the hand, into the day's clear shine.

The grove is budding in the ringing song
of birds, you seem to hear a call that sounds
from willows and the golden-gleaming pond;
it may be that the spring has been pronounced.

You're almost moved to answer: raise a cheer
to heaven, as if to the yonder-strand—
there is a touching touch, a squeezing squeeze,
as if a kindly spirit shook your hand.

Unmoving, time forever races: flies.
A breeze is shuffling air about the set.
How clear and shining is the midday tide!
Autumn lies many mellow days ahead.

* * *

The child has paused forever by the gate
and scampered off—forever, a small boy.
He'll grow to raise a roar and then abate,
he'll roam and love and taste a crumb of joy,

stand here, grow old, have children of his own;
he'll preen himself and, in a thin year, starve;
and live; and stare into the nights with hope,
grandfather though he is, to fly to stars

on freedom's wings; he'll stand here; sunk in thought
he'll muse at snow; he'll stand before himself;
toothless, he'll munch at pointlessness and pour
time in his glass; and never, always, then,

be more remote than any stretch conceived;
he'll lie upon his bier, a cold deaf clay
—the hall steeped in the scent of somber wreaths—
and stand, a boy, forever by the gate.

* * *

Bright dots of fireflies and lukewarm dark
— on grown-ups, pouring for themselves more wine,
the moon's half-crescent spreads a scanty shine—
the wind of love is breathing through the yards,

I sense and recognize it, still a lad;
and, picking full-blown lilac blossoms, start
a whispered letter, writing in my heart
to her, my unknown, how alone I am

and that I love her now and once for all.
        — Gone are the garden and the house,
but sometimes the accordion still sounds
to conjure up the fragile evening fall;

perhaps that's why there quivers in my eye
a silent sadness when, before I fold
you in my arms, I hug your shoulders close
— a sadness as if from a smothered sigh—

—————————.

* * *

A day like other wilted autumn days;
beneath the sky hangs silence—a dull whine
which, ever fading, never fully fades;
a hurt that heals with the proverbial time.

The gypsies plodded on with horse and cart
to the horizon, azure-tinted hills
—with tattered brollies carried under arms
but shoes like new ones, gleaming to the tips—

and I recall a sheep-dog with a limp
and, then, the suddenly deserted road,
the emptied air—and, for the briefest glimpse,
a red glow reigning in its live coal gold—

and then—again, forever—nothing else—
A boy, his heart sunk deep in thought to see
how time slips off, is resting silently
his brow on the deserted evening's edge.

* * *

Large hips and lovely legs, a voice that shades
to dusk—she might have both made love just now
and never yet at all; a childlike grace;
a smallish village, our native town

in Sunday calm; an ageing pair, we tread
—like ageing shoes: a pair, both one and two—
a creature birthed beneath the sky for good,
a gift, with compliments, to Life from Death;

onward we walk, a song not written down
by gusts of wind and never sung by snows,
young gods; by Simply Being held spellbound,
we are a searing shriek with muffled tones,

a creamy swish of silence pent inside;
we are the empty air which—no, *who* goes
as promise down the endless gleaming roads,
disguised as a plain painting: man and wife.

* * *

This afternoon, befuddled by the wine,
I dozed off in my garden. My bare feet
went tramping through the sky; a parakeet,
the breath of memory, perched close behind

my ear to whisper of pornography,
so that the bees came settling on my lips
to feast upon my smile, while cloudgirl wisps
were blushing in their innocence at me.

I woke up when the gentle sun declined
behind the hills and when an iron freeze
—like fire on a wound—reached in my shirt:

above, a deep and empty universe
had already sucked every bird inside
and, gaping, hung enormous over me.

* * *

In early April come the haywire days:
the salty southern wind, my mate of old,
the prankster that lifts mamas' skirts in play
and startles me by banging shutters closed,

and that plump sweetheart, my Chianti gourd,
saw me this morning from the tavern home—
in case my knees gave way, and making sure
that songs would roll with gusto from my throat.

We halted on the bridge. A silver light
was gleaming on the river, calm, unstirred.
I was more drunk on rapture than on wine.
The early bakers went about their work,

a wisp of cloud would drift across the skies
and an alluring no-sound from the bank.
"One never dies," I waved the thought aside
and knocked back—down the hatch!—the final dram.

* * *

A finger, stiffly pointing from the bed
away, and followed only by a child;
someone is soothing someone else: "Don't cry"—
the invalid now recognizes: Death.

A visitor, she smiles as if to say,
There, can you hear? the garden nightingales
are at their gospel-sweet romantic tales,
a hare is grazing clover on the plain,

a stranger's waiting for her love again,
beneath the bridge the passing river glints,
the harrowed fields are crossed by barefoot winds

and sparks have wreathed the image of a train,
and you—here, look into my eyes: you're mine.
Just bend your arm and let your fingers twine.

* * *

A picture from a passed and withered time:
beyond a hay shed teetering apart
a runty drayhorse pulls an empty cart
and close by, barefoot, plods a ragged tyke;

an unrelenting rain hangs from the sky,
a bird screams out—its name I've never heard—
the hour lingers idle and unstirred
on the dull edge of elderberry night—

I rest my eyelids for an arid flash
—and they are lapped by the lullbearing breeze
that tears across the river from the fields—
then wake up startled, blinded by my lamp

and shaken up as though I'd heard God's blast
into a lukewarm, starless, moonless night;
the picture plummets down beyond my grasp,
            beyond all second sight.

* * *

They look as though the gentleman had sat
by chance beside the lady in the chaise
and labored hard, as they rode through the shade
of trees along the drive, to strike a chat

but given up — the silence seems unstirred
not just by two but four, it lies so thick;
a clacketing and rattling on the bridge,
the younger horse, unhurried, drops a turd.

With every moment, life is slipping through
— the lady, thoughtful, gently nods assent —
and yet it seems to be forever noon

and never night-time, never winter's chill,
nothing but now, no past or future tense:
the carriage rolls along, the hour stands still.

* * *

A stone is glowing in the low soft light,
no silver piece, and slowly peters out;
the first of village windows flash to life;
the sun sinks down between two teat-like mounts;

in woods, the broadbacked wind has had its rest
and hit the road again; the quiet song
of girls, unhurried, folds into itself
and ceases but still faintly lingers on,

and all is as it's ever been — I'd shout
the unknown name of an unknown sweetheart
to shake the staircase, ancient and worn out,
which leads into the cold and purple skies,

but I've a mask I will not stir without,
and I'll not bare my heart at any price;
my gaze bent far beyond, I will exult
as I burn time and watch it turn to dust.

So to Say (2007)

* * *

What I believe in is the primal bird
in knickerbockers of an ancient cut,
pacing the farmyard where he preens and struts,
exalted by hens' cluck and squawk and stir;

and I believe he's—dubiously—right
when he crows from his dunghill to the sky
as if he'd burst in flame from sheer delight,
and then the dazzling picture fades a while;

he takes, the primal phoenix, long to wake,
as anyone who comes from nothingness,
and wakes up to himself and to the gaze
of choristers who cluck their praise of him—

I state my credo in the primal bird
—I, fledgling, all my life in swaddling-clothes—
my credo in his mighty primal word
by which he called me from his inmost throat

to be on the outlying edge of time;
in one who hones his beak on wintry ice
this side of parables, outside the orb:
a single peck, just one, and I'm no more.

* * *

All shall melt out: these evenings that you pass,
lit through by wine, sitting before your door,
and all that's ever come on you by chance,
all you have seen, not seen, or plain ignored,

all that you've missed or that has slipped by you,
it shall all pass. And all those other fates,
those never lit upon by any fluke
— both ardent passion in the southern blaze

and calmness of the Athonite retreats—
forgotten shall be all you've ever dreamed
and yearned for; wonder all shall disappear
together with your skull in nothing's sleep:

and yet when autumn rips the leaves from trees
and drives them, cold-disposed, in whirling piles,
a rook, high up, will caw you from its beak
into the lonely ear of time's grandchild.

* * *

I'm playing by the igloo, look, a Lapp:
the igloo's built of snow blocks, next to it
I'm modeling a podgy little lad
who is — am — holding a small snow-pressed brick:

the figure should be me, that's what I'd like,
a boy in fur who's modeling himself,
making believe it's mellow summertime
on a white evening when the shadows stretch —

a boy building a boy, just as I'm shaped
beneath your sealskin mittens into me,
my peer, now smoothing my — your — rounded face
— to give us recognizable full cheeks —

but now I've paused, to watch my hands and see
whether and who I am, and in what way.
Hey, big boy, what's that pause, you still with me?
I hear myself: he's humming at his play.

* * *

The poet's old, and weakness is a daze;
his hold has loosened and he now assents
that things are alien to their names
because the names have turned to things themselves;

no longer luscious beauties of the south,
the poems are mere skeletons, mere frames,
he stammers clichés, cries without a sound
—he who could always sing to please the taste—

into a shifting glimpse of trembling lines,
into a maze of interrogatives;
what death has pre-elected is his mind
        —and yet the more his wisdom lives,

a wisdom that does not build verse, that's true,
but still lights up the building work itself—
No shape, no clay, a wire hacked to shreds,
he hovers in the final customs booth.

* * *

The moon, a ripened red tomato, rose
behind the still volcano, fast asleep;
the outline of a murky fort, a moat;
a yoghurt path is beaten down to lead

— too narrow for a harness, you must ride —
through shallow mirrors of the heaven's plain,
and by the path a baby angel lies,
his rosy butt — you see it? — on display,

and now with soundless stomping there stampedes,
or so it seems, a herd of darks and shades,
is that right? which in passing almost raise
a dust cloud — in a trice they've disappeared —

to veil the light, as if a trembling stain
had spilt down on the early eastern side,
and the charm melts. Or could be that a sprite
has dabbled at his watercolor paints.

* * *

A second-hand bookshop: last night I leafed
through reproductions of some painters' works:
in an Impressionist paysage emerged
a soldier—tiny, only just perceived

in his blue jacket and his too-white pants,
a kind of knickers—from the dusky shades
which gather when the day begins to fade
and distance is transformed into a blank

corroding both the figure and head-gear
with all the surety of an eve drawn near,
he stood there, I remember, as is meet
for dashing soldiers, stood and did not kneel

—the heaven's vault above glowed murkily
in the last mystery, and grew coal-dark—
It was a soldier in parading garb,
already buried to the very knee.

* * *

The north, in winter, early turns to night.
Fat candles have been lit throughout the house
and over them keeps watch an unknown draft,
to drive each flame into a trembling fright.

The colonel with his young wife sits at home
into an afternoon like early night,
the lady's shoulders covered with a stole
— the fact is that the stove will not heat right —

she knows more than her husband thinks, knows all:
"You're dueling for me tomorrow. Scared?"
My glance recoils and sweeps the gloaming hall
to touch the rosary I hold in hand,

and I think of a rather snide remark:
"Who will you cry for, then, my faithless wife?"
"The one who will be dead," she smiles and starts
to wipe her glasses with a napkin, white.

* * *

By definition god can never die,
undying is thus everything he sees:
the sky, the sea, the olive trees, the vines,
undying you who dig there underneath,

undying is the wife by whom you rest,
your son inside her womb, a pea of slime,
undying all the fish caught in the nets,
the coming night — and may your rest be light! —

the crescent's gloaming and the starry glint,
undying under almond trees the goat,
undying is the flea that eats off him,
the worm beneath the tree bark in the grove,

undying is the coastman's weary rest
laid in the salt of dreams in deathless bloom,
and what, undying, waits at dawn for you,
and what is fated for your days ahead

and for the time when — soon — rightonthespot —
aligned with the smooth sea you'll stand erect,
        decked out in shallow soil and rock,
a deathless candle lit beside your head.

* * *

The aged dog is gone. Gone is the brute
who used to roll before the fireplace,
beg standing on his hind legs, drip his drool
      and pant and send the guests in gales

of laughter, imitating whining curs;
          the master is no more,
who always would address him as *milord*
—and, they said, introduce him as an earl—

the house has been devoured by arcades,
by vaults and porticoes, all caved inside,
the line is finished and the order changed,
the oak is brought to rot, the grapevine dried,

    all's past. Indeed, some winter's night
the traveler may freeze in his mid-stride
as if he heard a panting far and close,
but when he listens, only falling snow.

* * *

Where dusting snow is buried in its drift
as soon as footsteps wander off elsewhere
(there is no track, and none to follow it:
        the wolves are sleeping by the bears),

a solitary shyness treads through trees.
        She pauses on the clearing's edge
and breathes in, in her nostrils, in herself—
        she's found her way to being free,

                she stands as still as rocks,
a perfect painting: who had eyes to see
would note how rapidly her muzzle throbs,
note in her eyes a fevered lustful gleam—

and at the hissing shot, a drop, a trace
of bright blood on the bosom of the doe;
and just before she topples in the snow,
she soars high up into the open space.

* * *

I know that God will unsuspecting watch
at midnight the inn's door when I appear,
        revived by a substantial meal,
and, weakened by the bounty of the crop,

continue down along the human path;
He trusts me if I'm lured by the appeal
of red lights and the sweet call of the harp
— and let the podgy madam strike a deal —

He trusts me when I hail a taxi, hoarse,
to toss away my last cents like a king,
He trusts my bitter war with nothingness,
supporting me in our common cause —

well may I weave and wobble as I plod
                on heavy feet: so what?
                He knows: when my time comes,
        I'll head back to my home, to dust.

* * *

An autumn day: the self-devouring gale
is leaping at the garden, ripping leaves,
and when our glances have been filled with grief,
he prances on, as if he'd been repaid.

A lonesome time: beneath the lowered greys
of heaven, one who's never loved now seeks
a name by which to call his loss, too late,
guessing at it in terse and hacking shrieks,

a name of embers burning on the tongue,
a name that's rooted in oblivion, deep
—here stumbles even thought, not only speech—
if he calls to a stranger's window one

he's never had, a wife—"You called for me?"—
he shakes his head and gives a senseless jerk
as if to point to that dark, flapping bird,
the name of resignation, of defeat.

Hundredtown (2007)

* * *

The square, the statue and the river's calm,
the jingling of the trams on city streets,
the town hall, white with spires, at its heart
— it's morning, noon, the shadows of the eve —

a footpath tiptoes through the facing gate,
across the hallway, slantwise through the yard
to dart along a back lane to the park
and cross into the suburbs; gropes its way

zigzag among the houses, rosebush plots,
into a murky wood — for no good cause
it mocks the straight line, tying into knots —
it sweeps before a benefactress' door

— she's badmouthed for a slut because she gives
so generously — up the sunlit leas
it clambers to the churchyard and turns past
the ancient smithy into winter's dark,

sometimes it's overarched by leaping deer
or flashed across by snails' dry memories,
or flattened, after hail, by tolling peals
where azimuths run short of their degrees,

and soon it burrows into layered rock,
afraid to wade through mighty river flows;
as soon as winds pile up dead leaves on top,
down come the falling, never ceasing snows.

* * *

Twelve silver spires to a white town hall;
an endless dragging noon before the bell
has jangleclanged time's measure and before
the town's returned under its silent spell:

now is it true or does it only seem
true to a straggler who has halted near:
before him has a scenery appeared
—as in delusions or in memories—

and when it scatters up, a void will gape
—in which some godlike spirit, with his wit
self-shattered, will but start to knead away
at the primeval rock wrought from his spit—

all round will spread a no-world, where the soul
will recognize, at last, its home sweet home,
where no-one watches, listens, feels; and breathe
as it folds silent on itself: "I'll be."

The dozen spires honed to spines, erect,
the gleaming town hall and the heavy case
which you set down so you can wipe off sweat,
and still the bell tolls midday, tolls away.

* * *

A table with a gentleman and lady:
unmoving, mute, the paper still unspread,
two cappuccinos served but both untasted,
and now they jerk in unison, attuned,

two robots rusted over, fish and bird:
she lights up with a flashing sulfur head
and the old geezer plops in sugar cubes
—as if they'd been remote-controlled to stir—

and, stroking his moustache, he spreads the sheet,
turning his mouth into a snout to peck
                with it at characters
and get them every one, from A to Z.

Her gaze on distant void, the lady blows
                distractedly away.
          Eternity, distracted, holds.
The paper rustles as dry water grates.

* * *

On city outskirts lies a park, quite big,
with all the trimmings: fishpond, ducks and swans,
a tea pavilion and a whirligig
    and always someone rambling on

    along the gleaming sanded walks
and wondering how, for all their twists and reels,
what lies ahead is always — at close call —
sometime, somewhere, the end. The scenery

moves on and shifts, the light director shines
the lanterns of the morning and the eve;
        what's still to be
        has long since flitted by,

        what is forgotten lasts.
"Dogs on the leash!" "No trampling on the grass!"
The park is at its loveliest, they say,
when lilac blossoms flood with early May.

* * *

First April week, a drizzle halts its pace
above a garden on the edge of town,
a window on the upper story gapes
and now a woman's let the curtain down:

with everywoman's whiteskinned hand and face,
perhaps a ring gem sending out a spark—
You snort, "She must be in the family way
and cheating on her man, some petty clerk,"

just trying to suppress the sudden pang,
its meaning all but hidden from your eyes:
how many future memories you had
but then received just one of all those lives,

the rest were whisked by others out of reach
            for all your days' eternity—
And, swindled, with this note you plod away,
who gives a shit, into the April day.

* * *

"Which way will take you fastest to the zoo?
Look, there it winds away through maples' gloom
to lions' roars, to eagles, capuchins —
one lifetime, sir, and you can have it licked;

but should your fortune really smile on you,
it may be that you'll never reach your aim
if you should stumble at a fussy school,
or fall love's victim in your salad days

— just when the youth comes to replace the boy —
or long to draw from pointlessness a point
but land a ticket for an awkward prize
and be transfixed by overwhelming light —

this here's a shortcut, sir, I'm telling you,
you pass through maples on a narrow rope:
a strapping man, his hearing finely tuned,
might be the first to clear it — who could know?"

* * *

The vault is crowded with the winter stars
                                        hung low;
        a new moon's risen in their arms:
is it an eyelash? Or a silver boat

                is bobbing on the heaven's sea:
                        the plankton stars, alive,
                        beneath the surface teem
                                like city lights,

sunk in the distant void since God knows when!
Who didn't raise his eyes? on leaving home
in search of freedom — driven still ahead
by flight and led by mindless hope to roam

the wastelands, snows and neverending seas,
to lift each rock and see what lies beneath,
and sometimes, from a cheap hotel room, eye
the worlds long wilted in the depths of time?

* * *

At times in the old sailor rises up
the boy who'd sail, a grown man, all the seas
        —as he announced to Mum
when he had, says the story, but four years—

who'd sail some time the overwhelming tides
of every ocean, deep and measureless,
and ever lick away his years—the dry
and salty brine—from cracked and peeling lips;

a boy he is, just setting out to live
in that wide world that crumbles when you're old,
a little boy with prospects, hopes, beliefs;
too much knows old age—no mere beard of snow—

beyond there lies a sea, more like a sea
than those now charted on seafaring scrolls,
and down those misty seaways never steers
a ship of living men to ride its rolls.

Uncollected Poems (2012)

* * *

The moon's white butterfly has soared
at dusk above the karstland stones.

A voice of mellow tones
sang deep, with unknown warmth.

It sang of love to seas
and shores beyond all reach.

The moon, the butterfly, white-bright,
flew, never stirring, by.

* * *

Time hanging heavy on His hands,
God sets out for the human lands.

"God," wonders a young novice monk,
"are You at all? How can I know?"
"Because you seek for me above
to welcome me in your heart's home."

"God," says a juicy little tart,
"by His gold thingy stands apart."
"One sign of many. But you know
yourself they are all made of gold."

"God," broods a cobbler, in two minds,
"now can He wear such shoes as these?"
"He'll wear just any shoes you please
so's He can walk when He don't fly."

"God," snorts a merchant, puffed with pride,
"a God who neither sells nor buys?"
God's face lights with a laughing crease:
"Because He has just what He needs."

"God," ask I, bringing up the rear,
"where will my poem go from here?"
He shakes His head and thinks a while.
"Where you'll be fooled to think is right."

* * *

Glinting on the river stream
lies the moonlight's silver gleam.
In the village cried a cock,
but the day is still far off.

In the shallows lies, asleep,
stone by stone as kin by kin.
Nothing comes but memories.
Nothing to take out or in.

* * *

Through years and centuries the saint,
worm-eaten, ancient, clasps his hands
in prayer, as one in a daze,
unstirring ever as he stands:

eternal trance is in his eyes,
his spirit has to heaven flown,
all that is left is vanquished vice
and on his brow, a trace of woe.

It's winter, on the plains outside
a still day shading into eve;
and then it seems, as if one sighed,
that something in the wood has creaked.

Couldbe (2013)

* * *

There came a letter for the snow princess,
sent registered, a palm tree on the stamp,
with date spelt out and signed and all the rest:
Leo the Fourth was asking for her hand,

offering her his tropic monarchy:
she'd yield all power, all the branches known,
and he, responsible to her alone,
would roll her joint on joint untiringly.

How come she's sitting tight when she should rise?
Why dither shilly-shally vacillate?
Shut-eyed, she's smiling like a prime bimbette—
        now why not post a hot reply

in northern lettering of icy lace?
Why not have snow on runways ploughed aside?
She's sitting with a smile portrayed for good
on well-known background—dreams of southern land—

while early evening swishes up, subdued,
through mango trees; her darling royal man,
enthroned close by, of *her* dreams while he nods,
and all the rest of that idyllic rot:

mere chance is better than a wish come true,
        more real than the act is thought —
and sweetest is the never-tasted fruit.
Our drawers hold such letters by the score!

* * *

The circus wagon rattled out of sight
into the rainy ranges of the west,
and she was gone with it, the faithless wench—
that wasn't what her patron had in mind,

and it feels lone to dine without the cheat,
and lone the cognac at the coffeehouse
across the street from the gendarmerie,
and loner still ring the piano's sounds,

and lone to walk into the rented flat
and pry through the resentful bric-à-brac
—yes, pry; he'd paid it from his pocket, right?—
which it had pleased Madame to leave behind,

he paces by himself the quay in dusk—
let drizzle drench his pate! for, after all,
he should have filched a circus parasol,
and let him watch out anxiously for thugs—

he sobs into the rain, "No use to bawl,"
and mutters to himself, "The bloody broad!"—
so lone that even grief won't chat him up
as loathing rakes his heart, an iron claw.

* * *

If angels really are foursquare in form,
as it has been traditionally claimed—
all of them, servants, heralds, men of war—
how could this be completely ascertained?

When such a kindly spirit specializes
in watching over youngest little ones
—you know yourselves just what a baby's faith is:
God is not nearly picturesque enough—

at night the baby thinks him and divines
                    —half lost in dream
—that he is spreading wings of silky white
                    with smiling mien—

and so the baby, just outgrown his binky,
will look him up and down, and think he's kinky,
and check again to rule out any tangles:
a cherub or a seraph he may be,

but still the sum of his interior angles
always amounts to three-six-oh degrees.

* * *

The finest town the world has ever seen
has neither thoroughfare nor square nor street,
  and nobody has ever built
  —a clinic, church, school, court or inn,

a jail, apartment, stock exchange or bank—
  there are no bridges and no streams
  and—prick up carefully your ears—
  no soul, a woman or a man,

no cats, no dogs, no pigeons, flies or rats,
no bustle, no rush hour, traffic lights,
no city council—and it never meets—
and there's no sky or air or any ground

made out of sand or faith or rocky mound.
Just empty sea for seven hundred miles.

* * *

The wagon-driving woman calls to mind,
one starry night, still other skies and stars:
another horse had measured then the miles
of other roads in other steps and yards,

the dawn traced out still other towns to greet
the eyes of both, their skylines lined with gold,
another winter stung with other cold,
the year was nineteen hundred six and three,

and all was different and a different ring
was in the laughter from a roadside inn;
the cart was sometimes pulled by a huge cat
and rarely did the harness touch the track;

a different blue lay then on distant fields
of other kingdoms, other continents,
and, doubly other, is recalled with grief
and in the memory of someone else.

* * *

A man and woman walking off, entwined,
      seem from a distance to be squeezed
      into a single lonesome beast,
and when they can no longer be beheld

      through withered years now long gone by—
      before your eyes may flash a scene:
      once after dinner, by the sea,
         uncaught in heaven's webs,

      a star hung low in firmament
              one sudden moment
      will flash in a presentiment
and topple closer, closer, and still closer.

* * *

It's autumn, you are sitting with a book
—beneath the olives lies a promenade,
a tiny sea and idle sluggish waves,
a screaming gull is fishing in the blue:

say you've returned after a score of years
and all is as it's burnt in memory,
you're sitting as you pictured once this scene
        and waiting for your dear wife here,

she must have been delayed not far away
—perhaps with a more handsome gentleman?
it couldbe, rather, she has bent her gaze
                on shallows and the strand—

you're sitting, then, with a book tucked away,
a seaside bench, a late September day.
Above the olives rings a donkey's bray.
The wife is coming. She's been given grapes.

* * *

Over the town lies still another town
and where the town hall stands, there stands one more,
the picture has been neatly copied down,
each cross as cross, all gold ones made of gold:

in two eternities they glow from spires
which bore into the night skies overhead,
through both a like—not selfsame—winter spreads,
just like one painting mirrored in another;

two railway stations flaunt a fountain each:
        each fountain boarded up
by the two mayors, so that nymphs, twice three,
would modestly conceal their naked butts;

where two black bridges span a river each
        —as if from hopes to memories—
two figures plod away through double heaps
into twin snowdrifts of two Christmases.

* * *

The fire's humming in the stove;
the autumn's stripped the trees with freezing blast,
the archgod of the sun in lakeside park,
who warmed the company but a day ago,

knows their cold and fear and languishes
      along with them, worn out, used up.
The day after tomorrow is to bring
      the fledgling winter's early fluff.

But here at home the stove is lit, I say,
and our tommy—Tiger—purring low,
one hundred cruises are we from the gale,
one hundred south seas pictured in the tome

we children leaf through, sprawling as we please
      on our rug of wool,
we're never powerless and never poor,
and it's been only . . . a great many years.

* * *

I know who in the village sells good wines,
I know a woman in a candy house
        who grants me every wish unheard,
I know the crowing of the village birds;

the time when the moon's crescent pales to day,
the time when the sun's gong sinks down in blood;
the time when snow comes falling, light as dust,
        the time of unrelenting blaze,

        I know the bell — the parish lord —
I know the sky above, which steers the course
of streams and fish, of time and humankind.
What I don't know is where the village lies.

* * *

There lies a land beyond a dozen seas
　　　　of wind and cold and memories,
　　　　and there, through sleet and storm, sails on
　　　　a sailboat built of airy foam:
　　　　past isles of void and gloom it sails
into the dark as time, unmoving, waits.

* * *

No-one has seen the slender pines
above the fields in sunlit hills
or that well-trodden path that winds
up to the shrine of pilgrimage,

no-one has been struck by the bell
with undertones of bitter gold
poured from the broken diadems
of queens who lived on farther shores—

and yet at times, when any of us nods,
it strikes us with our hearts' whole might
that our home's that distant spot
not found beneath the earthly skies.

* * *

The autumn's home lies here — lies far:
                the groves are soaked;
there's time, and silence, and the dark;
         few stars; a half-moon rose,

         across it sailed a cloud,
         the pond splashed a cold gust,
         as if, from rotten mud,
         one — you — might speak up, drowned.

* * *

Was this a seagull's squawk at skies of gold,
chasing the sun which sinks into the deep?
It's time the wanderer found a bed to sleep,
if there is one dug out for him alone.

* * *

Over an after-dinner glass
a sight forgotten is well-nigh recalled:
a handsome country chest stands in the hall,
a tray on it, with four fine pears lined up,

for each side of the sky one fruit.
The northern is a whiskered farmer's house
        —and should you rob him, you'll make good
if you will toil, like him, day in day out—

and in the western lies alone a lassie:
she's smiling at the thought of you just now
        and through her golden Venus down
                is strumming on her fanny;

and in the east, a warrior shot to death
        entrusts you greetings for his folks,
the hopes that a promotion lies ahead
                —hopes doomed to sizzle out;

the southern has a tiny puppet show
in which you have been featured as a clown—
polite applause, the spotlight switches off,
        goodbye and thanks you came along.

Poems from the upcoming collection (2017)

* * *

A girl walks through the marshes: long since gone
            and carrying a light.
Above is nothing, they have closed the shop,
nothing, though there should surely be a sky.

      She walks, one who has never been
                mother or wife,
she walks who has been raped, who has been killed,
and floats, unliving, over living slimes,

she softly walks, air-memory with a light,
walks, light itself, a pale spark there-now-here,
which bobs away and then advances nigher.
Should she to some stray wanderer appear,

he'll follow, as his brothers did before,
this hope of rescue down the pathless mire,
          returning to his home no more.
         On silent moonless nights will rise

           beneath the empty skies
a stifled glimmer from the peat, rise higher,
and beckon since it will not hide away—
why should it hide when she is dead, and safe?

* * *

How summer in late August comes to wilt,
how bubblepurls toss with the rolling swell,
                    foamfroth, to dip
            unseen inside the ocean bed,

how high the seagull circles in the sky
and how the wind has presently hushed down,
how man and man ashore are holding tight,
                    clutched into one,

and how a bell in narrow distance clangs
        —perceived not by the ear but thought—
and how before it drowns, the sun, ablaze,
                will stop and pause,

            and over the horizon hang
                    a fleeting age.

* * *

It must have happened at first light:
an eagle, white,
came hurtling at the sky
and in his flight
he caught the sun — as if he'd burst in flames,
outwhitening the white, outblazing blaze —
and over heaven's plains
spread in the blue
without a wingbeat sailed
beyond my view.

* * *

From that oasis which sees naked stars
—a trick— the farthest known to eastern man,
     sets out one night for eastern parts
a train of men and camels — caravan,

and plods a thousand hundred lifetimes east
through empty rooms and days and swelling moons,
swallowed by distance and still farther spewed;
the sand is white, is gold, is turned to sea

     and air, oblivion, thin foam.
And there it is at last that it will pause
and catch the caravans that went before—
so all who leave their homes arrive back home.

* * *

A plain of water where the moon, that loaf,
    is eyeing his parading suit,
an ancient wind is resting on the slope
      among the heather shrubs in bloom

and puffing, naughty as he is, to crease
the mirror of our honored satellite,
who will unstirring, genuinely calm
      speed on his way, aloof and high,

to leave behind the rolling rocky beach
         and cast a glance
at his reflection elsewhere, how it gleams
on polished surfaces of other seas,

      proclaiming eventide
    to other hills and silences;
though not at once, there always comes behind
      tomorrow's light.

MILAN JESIH was born in Ljubljana in 1950. In addition to his poetry, he has written plays and produced numerous translations into Slovenian from English and Russian.

MICHAL AJVAZ, *The Golden Age.*
The Other City.

PIERRE ALBERT-BIROT, *Grabinoulor.*

YUZ ALESHKOVSKY, *Kangaroo.*

FELIPE ALFAU, *Chromos.*
Locos.

JOE AMATO, *Samuel Taylor's Last Night.*

IVAN ÂNGELO, *The Celebration.*
The Tower of Glass.

ANTÓNIO LOBO ANTUNES, *Knowledge of Hell.*
The Splendor of Portugal.

ALAIN ARIAS-MISSON, *Theatre of Incest.*

JOHN ASHBERY & JAMES SCHUYLER, *A Nest of Ninnies.*

ROBERT ASHLEY, *Perfect Lives.*

GABRIELA AVIGUR-ROTEM, *Heatwave and Crazy Birds.*

DJUNA BARNES, *Ladies Almanack.*
Ryder.

JOHN BARTH, *Letters.*
Sabbatical.

DONALD BARTHELME, *The King.*
Paradise.

SVETISLAV BASARA, *Chinese Letter.*

MIQUEL BAUÇÀ, *The Siege in the Room.*

RENÉ BELLETTO, *Dying.*

MAREK BIENCZYK, *Transparency.*

ANDREI BITOV, *Pushkin House.*

ANDREJ BLATNIK, *You Do Understand.*
Law of Desire.

LOUIS PAUL BOON, *Chapel Road.*
My Little War.
Summer in Termuren.

ROGER BOYLAN, *Killoyle.*

IGNÁCIO DE LOYOLA BRANDÃO, *Anonymous Celebrity.*
Zero.

BONNIE BREMSER, *Troia: Mexican Memoirs.*

CHRISTINE BROOKE-ROSE, *Amalgamemnon.*

BRIGID BROPHY, *In Transit.*

GERALD L. BRUNS, *Modern Poetry and the Idea of Language.*

GABRIELLE BURTON, *Heartbreak Hotel.*

MICHEL BUTOR, *Degrees.*
Mobile.

G. CABRERA INFANTE, *Infante's Inferno.*
Three Trapped Tigers.

JULIETA CAMPOS, *The Fear of Losing Eurydice.*

ANNE CARSON, *Eros the Bittersweet.*

ORLY CASTEL-BLOOM, *Dolly City.*

LOUIS-FERDINAND CÉLINE, *North.*
Conversations with Professor Y.
London Bridge.

MARIE CHAIX, *The Laurels of Lake Constance.*

HUGO CHARTERIS, *The Tide Is Right.*

ERIC CHEVILLARD, *Demolishing Nisard.*
The Author and Me

LUIS CHITARRONI, *The No Variations*

MARC CHOLODENKO, *Mordechai Schamz.*

JOSHUA COHEN, *Witz.*

EMILY HOLMES COLEMAN, *The Shutter of Snow.*

ROBERT COOVER, *A Night at the Movies.*

STANLEY CRAWFORD, *Log of the S.S. The Mrs Unguentine.*
Some Instructions to My Wife.

RENÉ CREVEL, *Putting My Foot in It.*

RALPH CUSACK, *Cadenza.*

NICHOLAS DELBANCO, *Sherbrookes.*
The Count of Concord.

NIGEL DENNIS, *Cards of Identity.*

PETER DIMOCK, *A Short Rhetoric for Leaving the Family.*

ARIEL DORFMAN, *Konfidenz.*

COLEMAN DOWELL, *Island People. Too Much Flesh and Jabez.*

ARKADII DRAGOMOSHCHENKO, *Dust.*

RIKKI DUCORNET, *Phosphor in Dreamland. The Complete Butcher's Tales. The Jade Cabinet. The Fountains of Neptune.*

WILLIAM EASTLAKE, *The Bamboo Bed. Castle Keep. Lyric of the Circle Heart.*

JEAN ECHENOZ, *Chopin's Move.*

STANLEY ELKIN, *A Bad Man. Criers and Kibitzers, Kibitzers and Criers. The Dick Gibson Show. The Franchiser. The Living End. Mrs. Ted Bliss.*

FRANÇOIS EMMANUEL, *Invitation to a Voyage.*

PAUL EMOND, *The Dance of a Sham.*

SALVADOR ESPRIU, *Ariadne in the Grotesque Labyrinth.*

LESLIE A. FIEDLER, *Love and Death in the American Novel.*

JUAN FILLOY, *Op Oloop.*

ANDY FITCH, *Pop Poetics.*

GUSTAVE FLAUBERT, *Bouvard and Pécuchet.*

KASS FLEISHER, *Talking out of School.*

JON FOSSE, *Aliss at the Fire. Melancholy.*

FORD MADOX FORD, *The March of Literature.*

MAX FRISCH, *I'm Not Stiller. Man in the Holocene.*

CARLOS FUENTES, *Christopher Unborn. Distant Relations. Terra Nostra. Where the Air Is Clear.*

TAKEHIKO FUKUNAGA, *Flowers of Grass.*

WILLIAM GADDIS, JR., *The Recognitions.*

JANICE GALLOWAY, *Foreign Parts. The Trick Is to Keep Breathing.*

WILLIAM H. GASS, *Life Sentences. The Tunnel. The World Within the Word. Willie Masters' Lonesome Wife.*

GÉRARD GAVARRY, *Hoppla! 1 2 3.*

ETIENNE GILSON, *The Arts of the Beautiful. Forms and Substances in the Arts.*

C. S. GISCOMBE, *Giscome Road. Here.*

DOUGLAS GLOVER, *Bad News of the Heart.*

WITOLD GOMBROWICZ, *A Kind of Testament.*

PAULO EMÍLIO SALES GOMES, *P's Three Women.*

GEORGI GOSPODINOV, *Natural Novel.*

JUAN GOYTISOLO, *Count Julian. Juan the Landless. Makbara. Marks of Identity.*

HENRY GREEN, *Blindness. Concluding. Doting. Nothing.*

JACK GREEN, *Fire the Bastards!*

JIŘÍ GRUŠA, *The Questionnaire.*

MELA HARTWIG, *Am I a Redundant Human Being?*

JOHN HAWKES, *The Passion Artist. Whistlejacket.*

ELIZABETH HEIGHWAY, ED.,
  Contemporary Georgian Fiction.

AIDAN HIGGINS, *Balcony of Europe.*
  Blind Man's Bluff.
  Bornholm Night-Ferry.
  Langrishe, Go Down.
  Scenes from a Receding Past.

KEIZO HINO, *Isle of Dreams.*

KAZUSHI HOSAKA, *Plainsong.*

ALDOUS HUXLEY, *Antic Hay.*
  Point Counter Point.
  Those Barren Leaves.
  Time Must Have a Stop.

NAOYUKI II, *The Shadow of a Blue Cat.*

DRAGO JANČAR, *The Tree with No Name.*

MIKHEIL JAVAKHISHVILI, *Kvachi.*

GERT JONKE, *The Distant Sound.*
  Homage to Czerny.
  The System of Vienna.

JACQUES JOUET, *Mountain R.*
  Savage.
  Upstaged.

MIEKO KANAI, *The Word Book.*

YORAM KANIUK, *Life on Sandpaper.*

ZURAB KARUMIDZE, *Dagny.*

JOHN KELLY, *From Out of the City.*

HUGH KENNER, *Flaubert, Joyce
  and Beckett: The Stoic Comedians.*
  Joyce's Voices.

DANILO KIŠ, *The Attic.*
  The Lute and the Scars.
  Psalm 44.
  A Tomb for Boris Davidovich.

ANITA KONKKA, *A Fool's Paradise.*

GEORGE KONRÁD, *The City Builder.*

TADEUSZ KONWICKI, *A Minor Apocalypse.*
  The Polish Complex.

ANNA KORDZAIA-SAMADASHVILI,
  Me, Margarita.

MENIS KOUMANDAREAS, *Koula.*

ELAINE KRAF, *The Princess of 72nd Street.*

JIM KRUSOE, *Iceland.*

AYSE KULIN, *Farewell: A Mansion in
  Occupied Istanbul.*

EMILIO LASCANO TEGUI, *On Elegance
  While Sleeping.*

ERIC LAURRENT, *Do Not Touch.*

VIOLETTE LEDUC, *La Bâtarde.*

EDOUARD LEVÉ, *Autoportrait.*
  Newspaper.
  Suicide.
  Works.

MARIO LEVI, *Istanbul Was a Fairy Tale.*

DEBORAH LEVY, *Billy and Girl.*

JOSÉ LEZAMA LIMA, *Paradiso.*

ROSA LIKSOM, *Dark Paradise.*

OSMAN LINS, *Avalovara.*
  The Queen of the Prisons of Greece.

FLORIAN LIPUŠ, *The Errors of Young Tjaž.*

GORDON LISH, *Peru.*

ALF MACLOCHLAINN, *Out of Focus.*
  Past Habitual.
  The Corpus in the Library.

RON LOEWINSOHN, *Magnetic Field(s).*

YURI LOTMAN, *Non-Memoirs.*

D. KEITH MANO, *Take Five.*

MINA LOY, *Stories and Essays of Mina Loy.*

MICHELINE AHARONIAN MARCOM,
  A Brief History of Yes.
  The Mirror in the Well.

BEN MARCUS, *The Age of Wire and String.*

WALLACE MARKFIELD, *Teitlebaum's
  Window.*

DAVID MARKSON, *Reader's Block.*
  Wittgenstein's Mistress.

CAROLE MASO, *AVA.*

HISAKI MATSUURA, *Triangle.*

LADISLAV MATEJKA & KRYSTYNA POMORSKA, EDS., *Readings in Russian Poetics: Formalist & Structuralist Views.*

HARRY MATHEWS, *Cigarettes.*
The Conversions.
The Human Country.
The Journalist.
My Life in CIA.
Singular Pleasures.
The Sinking of the Odradek.
Stadium.
Tlooth.

HISAKI MATSUURA, *Triangle.*

DONAL MCLAUGHLIN, *beheading the virgin mary, and other stories.*

JOSEPH MCELROY, *Night Soul and Other Stories.*

ABDELWAHAB MEDDEB, *Talismano.*

GERHARD MEIER, *Isle of the Dead.*

HERMAN MELVILLE, *The Confidence-Man.*

AMANDA MICHALOPOULOU, *I'd Like.*

STEVEN MILLHAUSER, *The Barnum Museum.*
In the Penny Arcade.

RALPH J. MILLS, JR., *Essays on Poetry.*

MOMUS, *The Book of Jokes.*

CHRISTINE MONTALBETTI, *The Origin of Man.*
Western.

NICHOLAS MOSLEY, *Accident.*
Assassins.
Catastrophe Practice.
A Garden of Trees.
Hopeful Monsters.
Imago Bird.
Inventing God.
Look at the Dark.
Metamorphosis.
Natalie Natalia.
Serpent.

WARREN MOTTE, *Fables of the Novel: French Fiction since 1990.*
Fiction Now: The French Novel in the 21st Century.
Mirror Gazing.
Oulipo: A Primer of Potential Literature.

GERALD MURNANE, *Barley Patch.*
Inland.

YVES NAVARRE, *Our Share of Time.*
Sweet Tooth.

DOROTHY NELSON, *In Night's City.*
Tar and Feathers.

ESHKOL NEVO, *Homesick.*

WILFRIDO D. NOLLEDO, *But for the Lovers.*

BORIS A. NOVAK, *The Master of Insomnia.*

FLANN O'BRIEN, *At Swim-Two-Birds.*
The Best of Myles.
The Dalkey Archive.
The Hard Life.
The Poor Mouth.
The Third Policeman.

CLAUDE OLLIER, *The Mise-en-Scène.*
Wert and the Life Without End.

PATRIK OUŘEDNÍK, *Europeana.*
The Opportune Moment, 1855.

BORIS PAHOR, *Necropolis.*

FERNANDO DEL PASO, *News from the Empire.*
Palinuro of Mexico.

ROBERT PINGET, *The Inquisitory.*
Mahu or The Material.
Trio.

MANUEL PUIG, *Betrayed by Rita Hayworth.*
The Buenos Aires Affair.
Heartbreak Tango.

RAYMOND QUENEAU, *The Last Days.*
Odile.
Pierrot Mon Ami.
Saint Glinglin.

ANN QUIN, *Berg.*
Passages.
Three.
Tripticks.

ISHMAEL REED, *The Free-Lance Pallbearers.*
The Last Days of Louisiana Red.
Ishmael Reed: The Plays.
Juice!
The Terrible Threes.
The Terrible Twos.
Yellow Back Radio Broke-Down.

JASIA REICHARDT, *15 Journeys Warsaw to London.*

JOÃO UBALDO RIBEIRO, *House of the Fortunate Buddhas.*

JEAN RICARDOU, *Place Names.*

RAINER MARIA RILKE,
The Notebooks of Malte Laurids Brigge.

JULIÁN RÍOS, *The House of Ulysses.*
Larva: A Midsummer Night's Babel.
Poundemonium.

ALAIN ROBBE-GRILLET, *Project for a Revolution in New York.*
A Sentimental Novel.

AUGUSTO ROA BASTOS, *I the Supreme.*

DANIËL ROBBERECHTS, *Arriving in Avignon.*

JEAN ROLIN, *The Explosion of the Radiator Hose.*

OLIVIER ROLIN, *Hotel Crystal.*

ALIX CLEO ROUBAUD, *Alix's Journal.*

JACQUES ROUBAUD, *The Form of a City Changes Faster, Alas, Than the Human Heart.*
The Great Fire of London.
Hortense in Exile.
Hortense Is Abducted.
Mathematics: The Plurality of Worlds of Lewis.
Some Thing Black.

RAYMOND ROUSSEL, *Impressions of Africa.*

VEDRANA RUDAN, *Night.*

PABLO M. RUIZ, *Four Cold Chapters on the Possibility of Literature.*

GERMAN SADULAEV, *The Maya Pill*

TOMAŽ ŠALAMUN, *Soy Realidad.*

LYDIE SALVAYRE, *The Company of Ghosts.*
The Lecture.
The Power of Flies.

LUIS RAFAEL SÁNCHEZ, *Macho Camacho's Beat.*

SEVERO SARDUY, *Cobra & Maitreya.*

NATHALIE SARRAUTE, *Do You Hear Them?*
Martereau.
The Planetarium.

STIG SÆTERBAKKEN, *Siamese.*
Self-Control.
Through the Night.

ARNO SCHMIDT, *Collected Novellas.*
Collected Stories.
Nobodaddy's Children.
Two Novels.

ASAF SCHURR, *Motti.*

GAIL SCOTT, *My Paris.*

DAMION SEARLS, *What We Were Doing and Where We Were Going.*

JUNE AKERS SEESE,
Is This What Other Women Feel Too?

BERNARD SHARE, *Inish.*
Transit.

VIKTOR SHKLOVSKY, *Bowstring.*
Literature and Cinematography.
Theory of Prose.
Third Factory.
Zoo, or Letters Not about Love.

PIERRE SINIAC, *The Collaborators.*

KJERSTI A. SKOMSVOLD,
The Faster I Walk, the Smaller I Am.

JOSEF ŠKVORECKÝ, *The Engineer of Human Souls.*

GILBERT SORRENTINO, *Aberration of Starlight.*
Blue Pastoral.
Crystal Vision.
Imaginative Qualities of Actual Things.
Mulligan Stew. Red the Fiend.
Steelwork.
Under the Shadow.

MARKO SOSIČ, *Ballerina, Ballerina*

ANDRZEJ STASIUK, *Dukla.*
Fado.

GERTRUDE STEIN, *The Making of Americans.*
A Novel of Thank You.

LARS SVENDSEN, *A Philosophy of Evil.*

PIOTR SZEWC, *Annihilation.*

GONÇALO M. TAVARES, *A Man: Klaus Klump.*
Jerusalem.
Learning to Pray in the Age of Technique.

LUCIAN DAN TEODOROVICI, *Our Circus Presents . . .*

NIKANOR TERATOLOGEN, *Assisted Living.*

STEFAN THEMERSON, *Hobson's Island.*
The Mystery of the Sardine.
Tom Harris.

TAEKO TOMIOKA, *Building Waves.*

JOHN TOOMEY, *Sleepwalker.*

DUMITRU TSEPENEAG, *Hotel Europa.*
The Necessary Marriage.
Pigeon Post.
Vain Art of the Fugue.

ESTHER TUSQUETS, *Stranded.*

DUBRAVKA UGRESIC, *Lend Me Your Character.*
Thank You for Not Reading.

TOR ULVEN, *Replacement.*

MATI UNT, *Brecht at Night.*
Diary of a Blood Donor.
Things in the Night.

ÁLVARO URIBE & OLIVIA SEARS, EDS., *Best of Contemporary Mexican Fiction.*

ELOY URROZ, *Friction.*
The Obstacles.

LUISA VALENZUELA, *Dark Desires and the Others.*
He Who Searches.

PAUL VERHAEGHEN, *Omega Minor.*

BORIS VIAN, *Heartsnatcher.*

LLORENÇ VILLALONGA, *The Dolls' Room.*

TOOMAS VINT, *An Unending Landscape.*

ORNELA VORPSI, *The Country Where No One Ever Dies.*

AUSTRYN WAINHOUSE, *Hedyphagetica.*

CURTIS WHITE, *America's Magic Mountain.*
The Idea of Home.
Memories of My Father Watching TV.
Requiem.

DIANE WILLIAMS,
Excitability: Selected Stories.
Romancer Erector.

DOUGLAS WOOLF, *Wall to Wall.*
Ya! & John-Juan.

JAY WRIGHT, *Polynomials and Pollen.*
The Presentable Art of Reading Absence.

PHILIP WYLIE, *Generation of Vipers.*

MARGUERITE YOUNG, *Angel in the Forest.*
Miss MacIntosh, My Darling.

REYOUNG, *Unbabbling.*

VLADO ŽABOT, *The Succubus.*

ZORAN ŽIVKOVIĆ , *Hidden Camera.*

LOUIS ZUKOFSKY, *Collected Fiction.*

VITOMIL ZUPAN, *Minuet for Guitar.*

SCOTT ZWIREN, *God Head.*